Simplified Astrology

Volume One

Simplified Astrology: Volume One

Copyright © 2021 Mark D. Meyer

All rights reserved. No portion of this book may be reproduced, stored in a retrieval system, or transmitted in any form or by any means, without expressed written permission of the author/publisher.

A reviewer however, may quote brief passages in a review to be printed in a newspaper, magazine, or journal.

www.simplifiedastrology.com

Cover Design: *Flammarion Engraving* (Colorized) - Artist Unknown

Celestial Sun and Moon - Sandersartgallery
www.deviantart.com/sandersartgallery

Table of Contents

Introduction	**6**
The Principle of Correspondence	10
The Principle of Vibration	13
The Principle of Polarity	14
The Principle of Rhythm	15
Cause and Effect	16
Free Will & Choice	17
How Astrology Works	**20**
Levels of Astrology	23
The Astrological Chart	**28**
Elements of the Chart	29
Houses & House Systems	**35**
What Houses Signify	38
The Twelve House System	40
First House	42
Second House	43
Third House	43
Fourth House	44
Fifth House	45
Sixth House	46
Seventh House	46
Eighth House	47
Ninth House	48
Tenth House	49
Eleventh House	50
Twelfth House	52
House Systems	54

Simplified Astrology - 3

The Planetary Bodies — 57
The Luminaries — 58
The Sun — 61
The Moon — 63
Mercury — 66
Venus — 70
Mars — 72
Jupiter — 74
Saturn — 76
Uranus — 79
Neptune — 82
Pluto — 84
Chiron — 86
North & South Node — 91

The Zodiac Signs — 94
The Elements — 96
Modalities — 104
Duplicity — 105
Planetary Rulership — 106
Aries — 109
Taurus — 111
Gemini — 113
Cancer — 115
Leo — 117
Virgo — 119
Libra — 121
Scorpio — 123
Sagittarius — 125
Capricorn — 127
Aquarius — 129
Pisces — 131
Decans or Decanates — 133

Simplified Astrology - 4

Tables of Correspondence	**135**
Reading The Chart	**142**
Aspects	148
Conjunction	150
Opposition	151
Square	152
Trine	154
Sextile	155
Minor Aspects	156
Aspect Patterns	**158**
T-Square	159
Stellium	160
Grand Trine	161
Yod	162
Synastry	**165**
Transits	**173**
The Lunar Cycle	175
Moon Void of Course	181
Planetary Hours	184
Acknowledgements	188
About The Author	190

Simplified Astrology - 5

Introduction

It must be stated that astrology is one of the oldest (and most misunderstood) sciences known to man. Every culture in recorded history has practiced some form of astrology. In some cultures, astrology actually predates agriculture. In fact, the moon phases and solar cycles *still* tell us when to plant our crops. While at large, we no longer live in an agricultural society, there is still nothing new under the Sun.

Astrology is an *infinitely huge* world. My aim with this book is to familiarize you with the working parts of this study and not overload you with things that aren't useful. The tools are in here and I will show you how they work. Whether you are an adept or an absolute beginner, I'm sure you'll find something here that you can apply for your benefit.

With the nature of our ever-changing and developing world, the last word on astrology will *never* be written. Given its age alone, the amount of pre-existing astrological literature is *also huge.* There is *so much information,* it can actually be difficult to get started. Everyone will have a different opinion or approach, naturally. To make this easy, we should level the playing field.

Simplified Astrology - 6

Let's talk about what astrology *is* and *isn't* so our expectations are in the right place.

Many people who come to astrology on a surface level are either looking for entertainment, self-discovery, a way to predict the future, or some indication of whether or not they can have a fruitful relationship with so-and-so. While astrology *can* assist with all of these things, it is irresponsible and irrational to try to do so without a functional understanding of the science first. The word *science* is used emphatically because astrology aims to observe, identify, describe, & explain natural phenomena. Astrology at large is a tool (and a Swiss-Army knife at that). As our understanding of the tool grows, so do the tool's uses.

"But Mark! Don't you mean *astronomy*?" No, not quite. In the past, astronomy and astrology were one in the same. Our modern scientific method has created a gap in understanding and therefore a disconnect. Truly, they are two sides of the same coin. To demonstrate this point, we need to discuss *science.* There are soft sciences and there are hard sciences. Broadly speaking, hard sciences (such as biology, physics, geology) deal with nature and things that are concrete, empirical, measurable, and exact. Soft sciences (such as sociology, psychology, political science) are not as rigid in their delineation, and pertain to humanity on a broad spectrum. Astrology is technically a soft *and* a hard science.

To practice astrology, a rudimentary understanding of astronomy is needed. *All astrological events are astronomical events, but not vice versa.* Astronomy is mostly concerned with the cataloging of celestial bodies. Astrology takes this a step further and looks at how humanity is affected collectively. We owe so much to the empirical thought process, but please understand that not everything can currently be measured. We are going to leave this point for now, as it's not a fun point to make, but a necessary one.

In the simplest and broadest sense, astrology is all about communication. Check the etymology! Astrology (From the Greek "Astro" meaning star; and "logos" meaning logic, reason, or philosophy) literally means *star language*. This is the study of how the stars, planets, and celestial bodies communicate with each other and life at large. Unlike any other language, the influences are expressed solely energetically.

The question then becomes, "how do we speak the language?" and not "is this stuff even real?" I promise it's real. If you still don't believe me go outside and look up! You'll see stars! And if you don't, you'll see light coming from *somewhere*!

Simplified Astrology - 8

Even though we consciously know and intuitively understand this, it is worth the reminder that *everything is energy.* There is quite literally *nothing* that *isn't* energy. Even the 99% of light that we can't see with the naked eye is still energy (and there is more *unseen* than *seen*). I am energy. You are energy. The stars are energy. The planets are also energy. All of our energies are interconnected and influence each other. This was not news to the ancients, so hopefully this doesn't come as a surprise to you.

To build onto our solid foundation, let's touch on a few other things that the ancients were aware of. Before we observe the stars and planets, we should have the correct mentality. There is much to be said about the Hermetic Principles, so we will analyze a few of the most relevant ones briefly. These principles will help us bridge the perceived gap between astrology and astronomy. I am all for the advancement of science, however there is still *nothing new under the Sun.* The ancient wisdom is here to remind us of what we already know. All of these can be found in *The Kybalion;* a modernized Hermetic text for those who are ready for it (and don't feel like reading emerald tablets). Without further ado, let's learn the rules so we can play the game.

Simplified Astrology - 9

The Principle of Correspondence

As above, so below. As below, so above. These phrases hold more meaning the longer you allow them to sit inside your mind. In terms of dimensionality, there are levels to the reality we live in. We generally spend most time perceiving the physical aspect of reality. Meanwhile in this 3rd dimension: there are other layers, such as the etheric, emotional, astral, mental, psychic, etc. overlapping the physical. In many schools of thought, our souls exist in all of these layers simultaneously, regardless of if we are aware of them.

While there are inherent differences in the planes or levels of reality, we can draw distinct similarities between them. This is what the principle of correspondence is all about. *Seeing an iceberg above the water indicates there must also be something below.* By understanding our physical reality, we are able to gain an understanding of the higher realms of existence. Again, everything is just energy. Each level is connected to *all of the other levels.* The work we do on this (physical) plane will directly affect the planes above and below. The work we do on the planes above and below, will directly affect this one (again, the physical).

I know what you may be thinking. "Makes sense. A little woo-woo for me though". It definitely can sound a bit "out there". So let's demonstrate this principle physically then. Take a look at yourself, and the atoms that make up your body. If you remember from science class, these atoms are made of smaller, subatomic particles. While I don't claim to be a chemist, I can tell you it is widely accepted that these atoms are made up of a nucleus in the center, and electrons flying around the nucleus in orbit. These particles make you who you are. To take this even further, quantum physics will tell you that your body is over 99% empty space. You aren't as solid as you think you are!

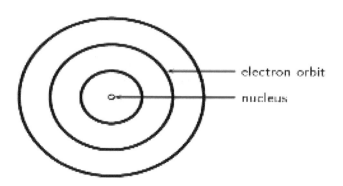

Now let's take a step back. A few steps back, actually. Past your body and past this solar system. In our heliocentric view of the Universe, the star in our solar system (the Sun), acts as a gravitational center for the other planetary bodies. Due to its mass, the planets make their orbital patterns around the Sun, each with varying speeds. Correspondence also tells us that this is the norm for the other solar systems in our Universe.

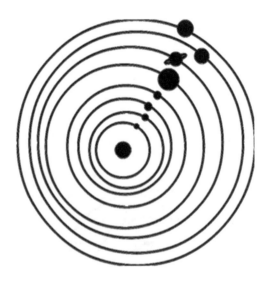

By now, you should be able to connect the dots. Our human bodies are the microcosm. Outer space and our solar system is the visible part of the macrocosm. There are levels above, below, and in between. Our connection to the larger planetary bodies is through our physical body. Vice versa, our relationship to our own bodies can be observed through the solar system.

We're getting a bit *twelfth house* here (more on that later), so before we go back to empirical I want to mention one more thing. For those familiar with the chakra system, and the bodily energy centers, correspondence will come into play here as well when we start talking about the planets in detail.

The Principle of Vibration

Simply put, nothing in our Universe rests. *Everything moves, everything vibrates.* You probably heard this in science class also. In your study of astrology, it is imperative to remember that motion and change are the only constants in this world. Every star and planet is in motion. Even when you sit physically still, your atoms will not stop moving.

The key points of this principle are *rate* and *change*. If everything is in a constant state of vibration, we can measure things based on *frequency, or the wavelength of the motion*. In some aspects, we are able to measure frequency physically. Subtler energies may be perceived and measured solely mentally, emotionally, or psychically. By being aware of this principle, one

Simplified Astrology - 13

can differentiate their own energies from the energies outside of themself. We can also observe how one energy affects another.

The Principle of Polarity

Opposites are identical, just varying in degree. Allow that to marinate within your mind as well. Everything has two poles; a pair of opposite qualities and many degrees in between. Let's think about it in a physical sense. Up and down. Hot and cold. East and West. Diametric opposites have many degrees in between. Each pole shows a distinct quality of the same measurement.

This principle offers profound insight in astrology. The zodiac belt can be drawn two-dimensionally as a circle. In the astrological chart, each of the twelve signs get thirty degrees of the 360 degree circle. Each sign or astrological house has its opposite six spots away. We will expand on this idea as we go on, pay attention to the opposites.

Simplified Astrology - 14

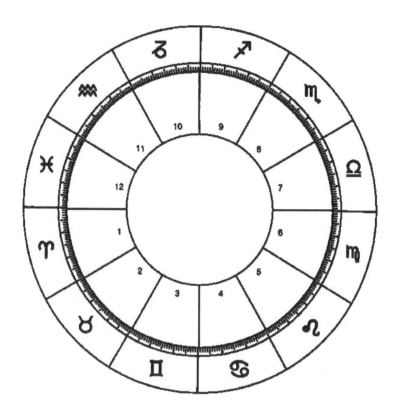

The Principle of Rhythm

Expanding from the Principle of Vibration, we see that everything has a measurable pattern of motion. You will see this in the planet's varying speeds of orbit in our solar system. Our rate of motion on Earth brings us around the Sun every year or 365 days. Each year contains twelve solar cycles (months), and thirteen lunar cycles. Our seasons last three months, from equinox to solstice.

Each day on Earth is twenty-four hours long. These patterns assist us in measuring the motion between the previously discussed poles.

The Principle of Cause and Effect

There is no such thing as chance or coincidence. Every person, place, thing, circumstance, or situation is the result of a cause. Common sense? Sure; but important nonetheless. Whether the cause is known or unknown makes no difference to the effect.

Things can get messy here for beginners with astrology. Focusing too much on the causes can complicate your learning process and stunt your growth. If you are a beginner, I implore you to start using astrology to analyze the past (effects) rather than automatically trying to predict your future or delineate how other people may act or feel based on their horoscope.

This process begins with obtaining your birth chart, the two-dimensional diagram of the solar system at the time of your birth. Through analyzing your own chart and past, you will be able to carry a greater understanding of astrology into the present and eventually the future.

Simplified Astrology - 16

Free Will & Choice

This may be the most important section of the book. Before we even begin studying this beautiful art, I ask of you: *get out of your own way*. It must be stated that self-awareness comes with responsibility. Astrology will not show you *what* you are doing or justify your actions; it will show you *how* you do what you do (and what you've always been doing). Extending from our last principle, it cannot be emphasized enough that you are capable of choice. Not only are you capable of choice, *you are always making choices.* Getting out of bed today was a choice. So was buying this book. Reading this book was another choice. Even indecision is a choice!

You will always experience change as a result of choice. Cause and effect, right? Now here's the tricky part. You are already aware of the effects you have caused, by and large. You are also living out many effects of which *you are not the cause of.* Your birth is the biggest one that comes to mind. There are plenty of other factors you can be influenced by and still not be responsible for, such as geography, climate, socioeconomic status, inheritance, etc.

Now what effect do you have on the planets in this solar system? None, right? Apart from Earth, it's a bit out of your hands.

So by now, you should be getting the big idea that it's the other way around. Humanity is collectively living out the effects of the energetic influences of the planetary transits while making our own individual choices. You aren't responsible for the transits (and that's okay! No one is expecting you to be).

Responsibility is *responding to your abilities* (kinda wild how the word explains itself). As you progress in your studies, you will realize that astrology *is* the cause of many of our effects. The planets can and will create change in your life, as they have your entire life. Being aware of the influences these planets and stars have on us is absolutely beneficial.

However, what *isn't* beneficial, is ignorantly assigning blame to astrological elements and throwing away your responsibility. This is where limiting beliefs and self-sabotage come from. Mercury retrograde is a prime example. We will expand on this phenomenon later on in this book; for now just understand that we experience this three to four times a year, *every year.* You will hear people blame Mercury for everything wrong in their life during these periods. These same people will use Mercury as their excuse for not acting on their responsibilities, creating new beginnings, or making the choices they know they need to make.

Simplified Astrology - 18

To me, astrology has always felt like mental gymnastics (never was good at the physical kind). This is akin to landing on your neck. Not only is this destructive to yourself, it's bad form and definitely won't take you to the Olympics. Be aware of "*I can't*" especially when it comes to astrology. Whether you think you can or you can't, you're right. Self-fulfilling (and self-defeating) prophecies are a gross misuse of the tool that is astrology. I don't care what planet is in your sixth house or how many squares and oppositions your chart has! Those have nothing to do with your choices.

When it comes to your birth chart and the placements of the planets within, you obviously don't get a choice. But when you have your roadmap, what are you going to do with it? Will you use it to justify why you can't have or accomplish the things you want? Or will you use it to learn yourself and leverage your abilities past the excuses and obstacles? That choice is totally up to you. The general consensus is: *if we know better, we do better.* However, this again falls on choice.

Simplified Astrology - 19

How Astrology Works

However remedial this section may seem, it is necessary to have a proper astronomical background to use astrology. Like I said earlier, the two really are one in the same, regardless of their slight differences. Seeing both sides of each coin will give you better buying power when it comes to your life.

This book is written from a heliocentric perspective of the solar system, and to this day, there are still those who wish to argue this point. Technically, there is geocentric astrology, but you won't find it here. The Sun acts as the center of our solar system, due to its gravitational force. Each planet completes its orbit around the Sun with varying speeds due to their size and distance. Astronomers subscribing to the heliocentric model will also debate whether or not the Sun is in motion. I urge you to look towards hermeticism for your answer (it is, just like everything else).

In the night sky, we are able to see stars from other solar systems. Groups or patterns of stars are called constellations. There are 88 officially recognized constellations at the time this book was written. As science advances, new stars are being discovered. Most often, these stars get grouped into the constellation they are closest to.

Simplified Astrology - 20

In order to start working with astrology, you need to understand *the ecliptic*. If you were to go outside and stare *directly at the Sun* (not recommended); your vision would create a straight line coming from Earth, through the Sun, and into outer space indefinitely. This imaginary line is called the ecliptic. What is important to note, is the group of stars behind the Sun that the ecliptic is touching.

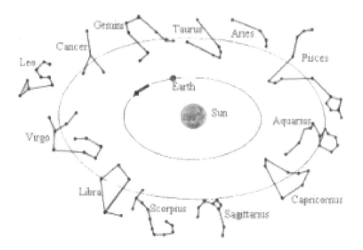

Throughout the year, as the Earth transits around the Sun, the ecliptic touches twelve constellations. This is called the zodiac belt. These are the signs that we are all familiar with. As you have probably already guessed, the ecliptic changes sign every month. What's even more amazing is that the movement of the ecliptic

Simplified Astrology - 21

corresponds with our equinoxes and solstices. The *Precession of the Equinoxes* is the official term for this process. This circular pattern is the wheel of our year on Earth, and our calendar is derived from this rhythm. Technically, the astrological New Year begins on March 20th (Spring Equinox), not January 1st.

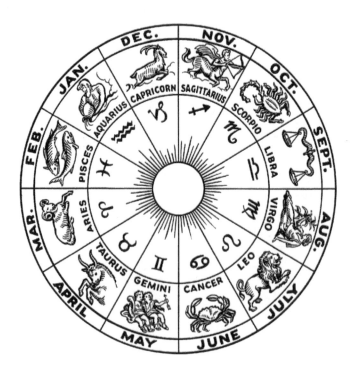

We already know physically that the Sun gives us life and warmth. The Sun also gives us light, or information. We are enlightened by the Sun, allowing us to *see* or be consciously aware

Simplified Astrology - 22

of the world we live in. Again, it's all energy. Although we cannot see the stars behind the Sun directly, we collectively live out the energetic influences of each constellation as the Sun passes by it (from our perspective on Earth). In fact, this is the same for every planet as they orbit through the zodiac. Each celestial body will filter the expressed zodiacal energy in a different way.

With our solar system's elliptical pattern within the zodiac belt, you should see how all of this falls into a circle. Circles (or astrological charts) are how we apply science and mathematics to astrology. I know I used the "M" word but please don't get scared. If you can count to twelve and do basic geometry, you can do this. By basic geometry, I mean telling the difference between a circle, square, and triangle. We'll get there, just stick with me.

Levels of Astrology

Applying astrology to your life comes in phases. As with most things in life, there are levels. Even disbelief and ignorance are part of the process. If your belief system is standing in your way, I cannot help you. At best you may find some entertainment here. I am going to assume you have a genuine interest in astrology; and once you get the knowledge you are going to run with it! As you progress and learn to love the tool, you will very likely come to levels past what I explain here. I commend you for that!

Assuming you have a compliant belief system for the work we are about to do, we start at *phase one*. This is the foundational understanding of the science we are using. That is what the beginning of this book and the subsequent chapters are for. Once we understand the variables that we will be using, we can move into *phase two*.

This phase is where we create a composite of the astrological elements. This is called the chart. You may have heard it referred to as an astrological chart, birth chart, natal chart, or transit chart depending on the context. These charts allow us to graph our solar system at any given moment. The amount of information and insight contained within an astrological chart is profound. You can create a chart for just about anything (yourself, friends, family, pets, relationships, businesses, etc).

The *third phase* is ongoing. I call this phase self-realization. This comes through analyzing your own natal chart. An accurate natal chart is the energetic blueprint you bring into this world the moment you take your first breath. Your

Simplified Astrology - 24

experiences in life will shed light on your chart and vice versa. As I mentioned earlier, as a beginner it is recommended to review your chart in retrospect. It is far easier to review your concrete past, than wrestle your conscious mind in an attempt to connect your memory with the present or future. You will eventually be able to do all three, but first *Know Thyself.*

The *fourth phas*e is what most people aim to use astrology for, and I hate to say quite incorrectly as well. I'm talking about synastry. Synastry is the study of interpersonal compatibility based on astrological elements. Sounds sweet, right? *It is.* The issue is, *most people don't know all the astrological elements!* Many of these people *think* they do, and this causes problems.

There is so much confusion when it comes to synastry. Frankly, the uninformed "astrologers" using synastry are a huge part of what gives astrology a bad rap. It doesn't take very long in a conversation with one of these people to realize they really don't know what they're talking about. If you think you understand a zodiac sign just because you had a bad romantic experience with someone of that Sun sign, I have some news for you. You need to move back to square one. Trust by the end of this book, you will be doing synastry the right way.

Simplified Astrology - 25

The *fifth* (and probably not final) *phase* is transiting. Studying planetary transits allows us to see how the movement of the planets affect us over time. To me, this is what it's all about and what we should be teaching in our schools. I like to call this *Metaphysical Weather Forecasting*. When you do this correctly, you can look into the future and know whether or not you need an esoteric coat, sunglasses, hat, or umbrella. Hopefully you can appreciate this metaphor.

Studying and working with transits *correctly* can become a circumstance where because of astrology, you *knew* better and therefore *did* better. Done incorrectly, this phase can also create circumstances of self-sabotage because you think you know how a transit may affect you. If your astrological efforts are negatively affecting your freedom or personal power, you probably need to go back to the drawing board and work on that foundation.

As time goes on, every planet in our solar system makes its way around the zodiac belt, each with a different speed. Not only does a planet's position inside a constellation affect the energy we receive on Earth, the geometric angles *between the planets* have an effect on us as well. Even the rotation of the Earth plays part in how the planetary energies are received. In fact, the rotation is one of the most important parts, which we will talk about later.

Simplified Astrology - 26

If you are serious about the study of astrology, I recommend you invest in an ***ephemeris.*** They are fairly inexpensive, and usually a once in a lifetime purchase. An ephemeris is a book of time-tables marking astrological transits. An astrological calendar, if you will. Most of these books contain 100 years of dates, as well as a key for reading the tables (however straightforward). There are also apps you can download to your phone serving the same purpose. This data is necessary for carrying out the fifth phase with accuracy.

When it comes to studying the transits, there is no better alternative for going outside and looking at the stars and planets yourself. That's how the old-heads used to do it back in the day, believe it or not. Please leverage today's technology for your benefit. But by all means, when weather and geography permit, go outside and use your eyes.

Simplified Astrology - 27

The Astrological Chart

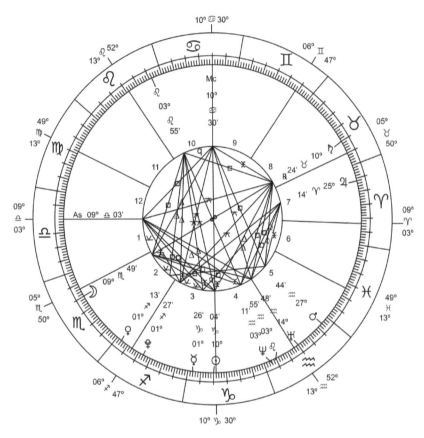

This jumble of shapes, symbols, and numbers is the composite I was mentioning earlier. The first time I saw my chart, I only dissociated a little bit! Sensory overload is definitely real so if you are slightly intimidated, I understand. I assure you, this tool is very simple when we separate it into its parts. The chart above is

Simplified Astrology - 28

only presented to you now to allow it to begin sinking into your consciousness. We won't start here. We will begin much smaller and build up to this.

The key takeaway I want you to receive before we start dissecting the chart, is that *this is a map.* More specifically, this is a map of the zodiac belt. Dead in the center of the map is a specific location on planet Earth. The middle wheel of the chart is used to show the rotation of Earth. While I can't tell you whose chart this belongs to (because I pulled it off Wikipedia), I can assure you the geographic accuracy matters *tremendously* when it comes down to interpreting the chart. The only thing that matters more than the accuracy of the location is the accuracy of the time in which the chart was cast. If there is an error of days to weeks in a chart, you will not have accurate positions of the planets. If the error is only a few hours to minutes, the horizons will not be correct. And of course if the location is incorrect, the horizons will be as well. Calibrate to the best of your ability for the best results.

Elements of the Chart

If you haven't noticed by now, I love arbitrary lists. With no intention of labeling (limiting) these maps, I like to compartmentalize them into *five* parts. There is much more to

Simplified Astrology - 29

astrology and chart reading than just this; however, these are the integral parts required to get started. The components are listed in this order intentionally, which may not make sense until we cover them all. The five elements of the astrological chart are:

1.   **Planet -** Pretty self-explanatory. We're staying inside the Milky Way also. *Planetary body* is a more accurate and encompassing term, as you will see our Moon, the Sun, and sometimes even asteroids in the chart. The word "planet" is widely used in astrology for brevity. Semantics. The planets inside the chart act as the metaphorical characters in our movie (life).

2.   **Sign (Zodiac Constellation) -** These are the groups of stars that create symbols within the zodiac belt. The patterns, shapes, and qualities of the stars imbue each constellation with a specific energy. As each planetary body completes its orbit, the energy it expresses will change depending on the constellation behind it (from Earth's view). The zodiacal signs represent the individual scenes in the movie.

3.   **House -** This is arguably the most important part of a chart. The word "house" in an astrological context refers to a position in the sky. This was the hardest part for me to grasp as a beginner. As a reminder, these charts are a two-dimensional tool to show what is occurring in our third-dimensional world. Even though the chart

Simplified Astrology - 30

may be, our planet is not flat. Shocker, right? There are different *house systems*, which we will go over. Every house system divides the sky from a specific location into twelve sections. It takes a full twenty-four hours for Earth to complete a rotation. Therefore at any given moment, six houses will be above you and six houses will be beneath you (and invisible, because geography). Again, this is why time and geography are important. *Accurate houses are a must.* To continue with our cinematic metaphors, these are *themes,* which we will expand upon later.

4.   **Aspect** - This is the geometry part. Very close in importance to the houses. An aspect measures the angle between two astrological elements (planet, sign, and/or house). Quick refresher: a perfect circle is 360° in circumference. All of our aspects in the chart will be measured between 0° and 360°, which are technically the measure. Due to this technicality, you will not see aspects labeled over 180°. This angle represents two elements sitting polar opposite from each other on the wheel. We do not count any higher to avoid redundancy. Aspects create shapes inside of the chart, which are very insightful when interpreting a horoscope. *A picture is worth a thousand words.* The keyword for aspects is *relationships;* as they connect different elements.

Simplified Astrology - 31

5.   Patterns - As we get into the details, you may notice this is really the same thing as aspects, except on a broader spectrum. Aspect or planetary patterns give us information on how the many relationships within the chart are connected, affected, and directed. These patterns are the *bigger picture* when it comes to analyzing the composite. Shapes, angles, and positions are all to be kept in mind. While it is truly necessary to understand the first four elements to work with patterns; they still offer much insight operating independently from them.

As the name suggests, this book is deliberately aiming to simplify astrology (more specifically, *astrotheurgy*). I assure you once you finish this book, not only will you understand the language, you will be working consciously with the intelligences of the stars. *That,* my friend, is astrotheurgy (*astro*: star. *theos*: god. *ergon*: work). You may have heard before in regards to language: *if you don't use it, you will lose it.* This remains consistent in astrology.

Many students of astrology get caught up in the memorization (and regurgitation) of correspondences and keywords when it comes to gaining an understanding of the planets, signs, and even houses. For many, this is a huge barrier of entry that prevents them from getting started. For this reason, we

Simplified Astrology - 32

have deliberately spent much time laying our foundation. The following chapters are designed to put the tool in your hands as fast as possible and get you chopping wood. For want of you to not waste your time and energy, I need you to *walk the walk* and do the work.

Memorization is necessary for the work we are about to do. I gently remind you, you're human. Humans come with limitations and boundaries. Learning is very similar to eating. Please remember to chew your food. If your head starts to hurt at any point during this book, this is your body indicating that it needs time to digest the information you've consumed. Allow the seeds ample time to germinate in your mind. The stars, planets, and your chart won't go away any time soon. This is not a race, please be patient with yourself.

Anyone who has read a magazine or newspaper horoscope understands the logical fallacy of trying to group an individual into one of twelve boxes. Before we expand on the elements of the chart, I want to illustrate in a very brief and general way, how horoscopes are *actually* created. It is so much easier (and more responsible) to do this for yourself, rather than paying someone *not* to teach you, but *tell you to trust them* instead.

Simplified Astrology - 33

As mentioned before, I don't intend to give you all the details right now (just allow the seed into your mind). Each of the twelve astrological *houses* in a chart represents an aspect of *human life*. Each *planetary body* represents an element of *the self, psyche, or individual* (and let's just say we're using about ten in our chart. Those numbers can get stupid when you involve asteroids). The twelve *zodiacal signs* are *qualities or modes* in which the previously discussed planets express their energy through. As a result of the Earth spinning *and* revolving around the Sun, each planet will have a placement inside a sign *and* house. If my math is correct, 12 x 12 x 10 = 1,440. Rather than just twelve, there's over 1000 different variables we can look at already. We haven't even mentioned the aspects, patterns, or synastry yet. Remember what I said about astrology being an infinitely huge world?

Creating a horoscope for yourself is as simple as obtaining your accurate birth chart, casting a separate chart for the time and place of interest, and analyzing the similarities and differences. This is a wealth of information compared to whatever crap you read from the back of *The Inquirer*.

Simplified Astrology - 34

Houses & House Systems

Wasn't this just listed as #3? Why are we starting here? Very good question, thank you for asking. Astrological houses *always* represent locations in the sky, relative to a precise location on the Earth. More specifically, houses are *the space around Earth.* At any given moment, half of the houses will be in the sky, and the other half will be below the planet (outside of your view). Earth is completing a full rotation every single day. As a result, every astrological *house* will have every *planet* and every *sign* in it, *every single day.*

We begin with the houses because they are *perspectives,* and not fixed elements. Houses offer a location for the rest of the elements to fall inside of. This is the framework for our chart. Before we analyze the rhythms of the months, years, or outer planetary cycles, we should start with the rhythm of the day. But how do you tell the difference between night and day?

Any way you answer this question has something to do with astrology. This is my favorite thing to ask those who think you can't be an astrologer because *they* don't believe in it. At some point: that big, bright ball of fire comes up from the horizon, does it's dancey-dance, and then descends back into *the other* horizon. It

Simplified Astrology - 35

has always been like this! While the Sun *is* in motion, it's movement across our sky is caused by the rotation of the Earth.

This is why your birth *time* is so important. The frame that a house system gives us is a circle (again,). Our day on Earth contains approximately 1,440 minutes. A discrepancy of even minutes will produce different degrees of the placements, and therefore *inaccurate results.* In an equal-house system, each of the twelve houses represent two hours of the day. For this reason, do not waste your time allowing more than a two-hour margin of error in a chart you read. Seasoned astrologers may consider that to be bad advice as a margin of error that big is far more inaccurate than a few-minute discrepancy.

I only present such advice, to encourage you to get started as soon as possible. Many people do not know their exact time of birth. Assuming you don't already know, the first thing you're going to want to do is text your mom or dad and ask them. If that doesn't yield the right result, pry a little more. What hospital was it? Was it morning or night when you arrived? And when you left? How long of a process?

Let's say that was a failure and your parents didn't have a stopwatch in the delivery room. The next course of action is locating your birth certificate. If this doesn't have the time, call the

Simplified Astrology - 36

hospital and request your birth records. If for some strange reason, this still does not yield a satisfactory result, you can always try divination (with a pendulum). If you need this explained, or aren't good at divination, don't do this!

If in the worst case scenario, mom and pop don't know, you were born on a bus, and the string-thing doesn't work: don't worry. You're going to cast a Solar Chart. This is a fancy way of saying "nobody knows what time it was". A solar chart will show you the map of the solar system, without the rotation of the Earth (and therefore no house system). For simplicity, most chart calculators cast solar charts at noon. Much less detailed, but still better than *The Inquirer.*

Simplified Astrology - 37

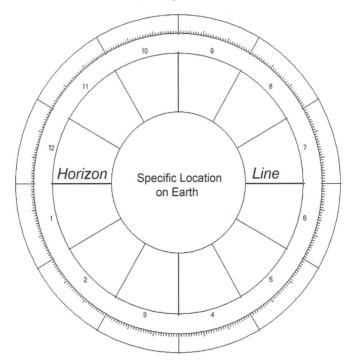

What Houses Signify

Before we discuss the systems of house division and how they are calculated, let's answer a very important question. When it comes to the chart, what are houses for? What do they do? What information can we gain from studying them? This is perhaps the most important question of all, due to the answer. Over time, many different house division systems have been created. The underlying theme beneath all of these systems is that the locations in our sky correspond to aspects of *human life,* or perhaps life in general.

Through careful observation, astrologers since the Babylonian times noted planetary bodies affect humans in similar ways as they aspect or transit through *certain areas in the sky* (the houses). The twelve-house system is a mental filing cabinet in which we can compartmentalize the different *themes* or *archetypes* that are consistent throughout every person's life. This is vital. Your astrological efforts will benefit your life *so much more* if you *overstand* (not understand) what life is, and what it can be for you. Without this framework, we truly can't expect to understand *where* or *how* astrology affects us personally.

Remember what I said about putting a person into one of twelve boxes being a logical fallacy? Now what if we put *one person* into *twelve boxes*? Sounds kinda messy. Maybe even illegal. Well that's the Circle of Life, my friend (quite literally). We have to do this. You said you could count to twelve, right?

The real beauty of all of this is that life fits *perfectly* within the twelve boxes. The boxes are arranged in a circle and even tell a

Simplified Astrology - 39

story when opened chronologically. Please keep in mind, life has changed dramatically since our astrological forefathers. For example, your ancestors may not have had a car, 9 to 5, or the internet. Everything in your life *will* fit into one of these compartments. As the world changes, astrologers must adapt.

The Twelve House System

Ironically, this is something I have found to be *oversimplified* in many astrology books. This subject does not need to be complicated, however there is much to be said. As you learn the houses, you may be able to notice similarities or themes between the houses and the zodiac wheel. I encourage you to make notes of any connections you may find as the correspondences will assist your memory. It must be stated, the houses *are not* the signs (and vice versa). Please understand that this type of delineation is a crutch. It will help you in the beginning, but hurt you later on if you keep doing it. Aries doesn't always mean first house. Eighth house doesn't always mean Scorpio, and so on. But still, this doesn't mean an Aries person *won't* display distinct qualities of ego (first house).

Simplified Astrology - 40

While we fill in the details of how charts work, I would recommend you have a notebook (or at the very least a piece of paper) to illustrate this for yourself. Reading this information is one thing, consuming it and recreating it is a whole different thing in regards to *retention of information.* I personally won't get anything out of you copying the diagrams down, but you definitely will. There are no rules to your notes. Feel free to add, subtract, and take what is useful to you. Find a pen and heed the Hermetic reminder.

Opposites are identical, just varying in degree. This principle will greatly expedite your learning of the houses and signs. Making the 180° jump across the wheel *should* create connections for you every time. The two elements you find on any pole will show the same measure, however on different ends of the spectrum. The first house will illuminate the seventh house. The second will illuminate the eighth. This pattern follows even from the sixth to the twelfth. I hate to call Hermeticism a *hack,* but learning six groups of elements is much quicker than learning twelve separate ones. Let's take it from the top.

Simplified Astrology - 41

The First House

Commonly referred to as *The House of Self.* The prerequisite of life is *to be.* The first house is all about you, and more specifically *what you are.* Your body, your physical appearance or constitution (especially facial features), and your perception of yourself all fall into this house. Individuality and ego are keywords. The first house represents the earliest stage of life in which you become aware of the world, yourself, and the separation of the two.

The first house always begins on the leftmost edge of the chart and extends downward in a counterclockwise manner. The line beginning the first house is usually marked "AS" or "ASC", short for *Ascendant.* Geographically, wherever you are, this line corresponds to the *eastern horizon.* The constellation in the first house at the time of your birth, becomes your *ascendant sign.* This is the sign that "ascends" first into the sky, relative to rotation of and location on Earth. You technically can't see the first house, because it begins on the horizon and continues underneath.

Simplified Astrology - 42

The Second House

Now that you *are,* there are some things that you're going to need to sustain your life. This house is archaically titled, The House of *Possessions* by most. You've probably realized the self needs more than just *stuff,* at this point. Your physical needs include (but are not limited to) food, water, clothes, and shelter from dangers. The theme here is *personal resources.* Yes, this would include all of your possessions (and all of your money too, as this is our modern means of getting what we need). Your second house is also tied to your *earning potential.*

Everything you own which has value fits into your second house. Even the things you *value* and *appreciate* in a non-monetary sense are found here because they contribute to your needs in some way. Bear in mind, your needs are not limited to purely the physical. The second house represents your immediate needs and your ability to fulfill those needs.

The Third House

This is *The House of Communication.* More importantly, the third house corresponds with your surroundings, or immediate

Simplified Astrology - 43

environment. Having properly taken care of your needs, you are free to learn, explore, analyze, and create your own ideas about the world you live in. You can share those ideas with the ones in your world.

Friends, family, and coworkers fall into this house. Here you can also find the places you go on a regular basis, or places in close proximity to you. Continuing with the theme of communication, the third house includes our cell phones and personal computers. Your social media timeline is also the third house. You can probably see how many things in your life will fall into multiple houses. Again, we have to adapt to the times and be mentally flexible. To drive the point home: I'm going to note that your car is also part of the third house (and second house), and *the walk to your car* is the third as well. You should be getting the idea by now. To recap, this is the realm of short-term travel (namely for work and education) and the exchange of information.

The Fourth House

To continue our narrative: now that we have taken care of our needs and learned to communicate with our immediate environment, we will begin to seek comfort, shelter, or some form of stability. This is *The House of Home.* The House house? So

Simplified Astrology - 44

what do houses *house?* Houses house people, pets, furniture, all kinds of things really. When it comes to the fourth house, this is the realm of homelife. Your family, relationship with parents, the people you live with, and the house you live in all fall into this category. Everything inside of a household as well as domestic *events* (not limited to issues) are found here. As our circumstances of home (or lack thereof) are inherited, the fourth house will show you at your most vulnerable. This realm includes beginning *and end* of life care.

The fourth house cusp is directly beneath the Earth, and therefore at the bottom of a chart. In a chart you may see the fourth house cusp labeled as the "IC" (latin for Imum Coeli, "bottom of the sky"). I find a more appropriate name is the *"I don't C"*, as this location is invisible from our perspective. Jokes aside, this position is also labeled as the "Nadir" by some, it's the same thing. The fourth house's physical location also corresponds with its energetic theme of the *most unseen* or *most unexposed* aspect of the self.

The Fifth House

This is where things get *spicy.* The comfort of a solid foundation is what allows us to have *fun.* The fifth house is *The House of Creative Expression* (on every level of correspondence).

Simplified Astrology - 45

Let's think of some ways in which we express ourselves creatively. We've got music, writing, painting, sculpture, dancing, and *even sex*. Especially sex, as this creates children and families. This realm includes the family that *you personally* have created. We find your social life and the pleasures you indulge in inside of this house as well.

The Sixth House

The Sixth House is the refinement of your personal world. Often referred to as the *House of Work, Service, or Health;* this house encompasses a large portion of life. Not only are we referring to your job (or what you decide to do all day), we are looking at your *habits.* This house indicates the ways in which you direct your energy to be of service to yourself and others. More specifically, this is how the *physical body* is used. The sixth house in a natal chart will also indicate dispositions towards certain health conditions through placements or aspects. This is the same location that will indicate what skill sets one is likely to develop.

The Seventh House

I remind you, this is where polarity comes into play. You may have noticed the first six houses all have something to do with

Simplified Astrology - 46

the individual. The entire bottom of your natal chart (in terms of houses), is all about *you.* Make notes of the opposite houses and their similarities as we proceed. The final six houses represent the sky above the horizon, within our view.

The seventh house, also called the *descendant* due to its opposition of the ascendant, is the *House of Relationships.* The opposite end of the spectrum which is knowing yourself (1st), is knowing *the other.* Circumstances of relating to other individuals falls into the seventh house. This includes romantic relationships such as marriage, but also friendships, partnerships, kinships, or any other type of *ship that you and another could sail through esoteric waters.* Relationship is a beautiful, all-encompassing term for what the seventh house represents. Your relationships will illuminate what connection you have to those in your life. In other words, this connection is why the two of you *relate.*

The Eighth House

This is a house which needs not be oversimplified. Yes, this is the *House of Death and Regeneration,* but a whole lot of other things as well. Why is this the house of death? Death is the opposite of having our physical needs met. After all we have is taken away, the eighth is what is left. Physical harm or neglect

Simplified Astrology - 47

does not always mean death, however. Any living person can attest to the powerful regenerative abilities of the body, and *all living beings.* The eighth house in a chart indicates how we may regenerate or transform ourselves and aspects of our lives.

This house indicates *shared resources.* Investments, inheritance, gifts, mutual funds, joint bank accounts, credit, and even tax are examples of shared resources. The house you and your spouse live in falls into the category of *shared resources* too. This is the natural next step after the formation of a marriage or business partnership. Banking and finance are the world of the eighth house.

The eighth house brings with it the awareness of the limitations of health, the physical, and the material. In this way, funerals, wills, and the disbursement of property or assets falls into this world. There is much to be said (later) about the eighth house due to its planetary correspondences. It should be noted here, one archetype of the eighth is *recycling the material back to the spiritual.*

The Ninth House

To extrapolate from the third, we have *Higher Learning* and *Long-Distance travel.* The ninth house is the world of expansion and experience to create wisdom, rather than

Simplified Astrology - 48

knowledge. Wisdom is knowledge gained through *experience* which can *be used*. Knowledge is endless. Everybody knows things. The more you know, the more you realize you don't know (no ledge).

Within the ninth house comes the philosophy and mental structures of how our shared resources should be used and ideally *expanded*. Publishing, government, law, and philosophy itself is the realm of the ninth. In this area, we look at the collective thought-process, as opposed to the individual's. Travel, study, and new experiences are all pathways into the group-mind. All avenues in which we exit our immediate environment to expand and gain benefits or experience are found here.

The Tenth House

Physically, this is the sky directly above any given location on the planet. You will often see the cusp of this house written as "MC" (medium coeli; top of the sky) in the top of the chart. This point is also referred to as the "midheaven". The elements of the tenth house are best noticed through correspondence to the physical. The tenth is the same spot you find the Sun at noon, at its highest and most visible (consequently at midnight, the Sun is in the *fourth* house).

Simplified Astrology - 49

The tenth house is the area of life in which you are the most *visible*. For this reason, many refer to the tenth as the *House of Career*. A distinction must be made between career and job, however. Career is very close to *calling*, oftentimes what one thinks or feels they *should* be doing. A job is something you do for money or resources. Your job can fit inside of your career because the career is much bigger. The theme of career is also *what you would like to be known for*.

Placements in or aspects to the tenth house will impact your business (and the ways in which you conduct business), career, and even *social status*. The way you are seen publicly is written in the tenth; this is in direct opposition to the IC (fourth house). Above all, this house represents how you conduct your affairs (financial, personal or otherwise) in a public manner. The theme of security continues from the opposite house, however in a more *visible* and *encompassing* way.

The Eleventh House

This is a good time to reflect back on the other houses and what has already been covered. Our *self*, first and foremost, is where we started. We took care of our needs and secured resources. We've learned to communicate with our environment as

Simplified Astrology - 50

well as find comfort within it. This gave us the foundation needed to express ourselves, take care of ourselves and others, and build new skills sets.

The reflection of these elements birthed relationships. Relationships naturally came with the exchange of resources and ideas. Thus individuals collaborate, learn, build, and expand. And that's pretty much it, right? Looks like we've covered all of what life is.

But you gotta have friends! Friends, or some connection to a group is paramount to life. Humans are *pack animals.* Community, or at least a *sense of community* is what every person strives for on some level. Thus is the realm of the eleventh house. The eleventh includes the friends we make, as well as the groups we are a part of. We make friends and groups in the first place because these individuals align with our ideals or values. There are some groups that aren't as deep as that but it must be stated, the eleventh house encompasses our *hopes and dreams.* Here we find what we envision for ourselves and others for a better tomorrow.

The dichotomy of the fifth and eleventh house is a beautiful one. In the fifth, we find your expressions, pleasures, and your children. We find the same on the other side, except this time it's *everybody's children.* In other words, *everybody.* The eleventh

Simplified Astrology - 51

house is a look at the collective as a whole, and how *we,* collectively as well as individually, can express ourselves in a way that is beneficial for all. *Friends, dreams, group identity.*

The Twelfth House

I'm certain you know there's more to life than taking care of your physical needs and hanging out with your friends and family. You got questions. So do I, friend. I'm pretty sure we all do and in fact, have asked a lot of the same ones; perhaps in different words. *Why are we here? What's gonna happen when I die? What's the right way to live?* You bought an astrology book so we aren't even going to try to get into it. The only appropriate way to answer those questions is *it all depends on what you believe.*

Your *belief system* is a huge part of what makes you, you. Beliefs, which can be largely unconscious, govern all of our actions. It is not my place to tell you *what* to believe, I only wish to draw attention to the impact *your belief* makes on *your reality.* Many astrologers call the twelfth *The House of Self-Undoing.* This is appropriate, however confusing if not properly expanded. There are many methods in which the self is undone, not all of which are

Simplified Astrology - 52

centered upon belief. At large, the self is undone through our psychology.

Continuing the sixth house's theme of health and vitality, we see the twelfth reach into the mental and spiritual aspect of the self. In practice, harsh aspects to this house may indicate mental illness (such as anxiety, depression, or insanity), insomnia, addictions and bad habits. A well-aspected twelfth house would indicate spiritual and mental well-being, as well as mystical insight or channeling prowess.

Mental health, religion (or lack thereof), beliefs, hospitals, and prisons belong in this infinitely deep house. I vow not to force any of my beliefs upon you, however I will present my opinion (use as much salt as you like). *The far reaching effects the twelfth house has on the individual makes it one of the most important houses.* Remind you, we are in the realm of unconscious memory. This is the effect *of cause and effect.* Karma, if you will. In dealing with one's karma one may be self-illuminated or self-deceived depending on choice.

The connections to the spirit at large make this house one that should not be limited with words. Words actually are not an appropriate tool to describe some of the things the twelfth encompasses. To get your attention to the right edge of your mind,

Simplified Astrology - 53

I want you to think of *prayer*. Time spent in isolation or meditation. *Dreams* (the sleeping kind). Astral projection. *Psychic perception.* Spirituality. This is on the surface of the twelfth.

In the narrative of the wheel, the turning of the twelfth is the knowledge of life and its continuation or disbursement after death (be it true or false). All of us have a different idea of how this works. Again, that's what *you* believe (the world you BE-LIVING in). It's okay for us to have different worlds. One day, we will collectively learn to exist peacefully regardless if we disagree on where we came from or where we are going next. When the time comes, we're all gonna be too dead to care anyway. *So get excited!* With the ascendant coming next, you can conclude this is the area in which the Sun rises at dawn.

House Systems

It must be stated, there are various methods for calculating astrological houses. Before computers, casting a chart was done by hand with specific mathematical rules kept in mind. In this day and age, we can plug our information in and play the game without even necessarily knowing the rules. I won't bore you with the minute details of the various house systems, but I will draw your attention to what's important.

We have to keep in mind *geography* and the precession of the equinoxes. The Earth's tilt and orbit ensures the planets will not spend an equal amount of time in each house. If you really consider your own life - are your astrological houses completely equal? Chances are - they aren't. Before computers, equal-house systems were used almost exclusively. In short, an equal-house system makes all twelve of the houses the exact same size. It's easy to work with but scientifically speaking - we know this isn't exactly accurate. This type of chart casting is very effective at large, but has one major flaw apart from not being exact. It completely falls apart at extreme latitudes.

For this reason, many astrologers have opted to use the Placidus system - as it divides the houses based on geography and the Sun's transit of the sky. The underlying premise of the Placidus system is that the planets will spend an equal amount of time in the houses of each quadrant. Consequently, the houses will be different sizes. Depending on your geography, you may not even notice that they aren't equal while using Placidus. There could also be vast differences and intercepted signs. This concept is intentionally oversimplified here as extensive information on house calculation is no longer necessary to get started. Largely, Placidus is the most commonly used house system in Tropical

Simplified Astrology - 55

astrology. There are many different methods of house division, and each has its pros and cons. Given the bulk of information regarding each system - video lectures are the most effective way to dive into the specifics. We may cover this in Volume Two: *Deliberately Over-Complicated Astrology.*

The Planetary Bodies

Now that we've set the stage, it's time to look at the actors or stars (see what I did?) of our movie. It is imperative to have an understanding of the planetary bodies *before* learning the zodiac signs, as planetary correspondence and rulership play a part in the energy of each sign. You won't find extensive tables, charts, or lists in this book explaining what each planet does in each sign and in each house. Through the functional explanations here, you will not need them. Write your own list if you want. Better yet if you benefit from creating lists, please do it. Check the *Correspondences* section in the back of this book for help.

The *names* of the planets in our solar system are Greco-Roman in nature. The attributions given to the planets through gods of various pantheons are even older. The collective-conscious has built up massive amounts of energy around the names, symbols, and stories behind the planets. Mythology and physical correspondence (what the mythology is based on) is a well, rich in information.

We can tell much about what a planet represents for us *astrologically* by analyzing it *physically.* Again, this is where the rudimentary understanding of astronomy is beneficial. Every

Simplified Astrology - 57

planet, including our own, is in motion. Not only are these bodies moving, they are *vibrating* and radiating a specific energy. Fun fact, we can actually measure the vibrations of these planets and they each correspond to musical notes (you can read about this if you want but it's not relevant to the work we are doing now).

As each planet makes its way around the solar system, the energy it expresses is *modified* by the energetic patterns of the constellation (sign) behind it (relative to Earth). In addition to the constellation, the planetary energies are also affected by the geometric angles (aspects) between *other planetary bodies.* When a planet transits through a certain one of your houses, you will see those energetic influences in *that part* of your life. When we cover the signs and the aspects, you will be able to actually see this.

The Luminaries

As mentioned previously, not all of the planetary bodies found within the chart are *technically* planets. It makes the most sense to begin with the biggest and brightest lights in our sky. I am referring to the Sun and the Moon. Ironically, this is why your magazine horoscope never made sense. If your horoscope *did* apply to you, I promise it was vague enough to apply to *everyone.*

Simplified Astrology - 58

Your zodiac sign is based on the Sun. Our year's (360°) wheel closely corresponds to the approximate 365 days in our calendar. We can deduce, the Sun moves *approximately* one degree every day. This is why you can guess your friend's sign based on their birthday. Our equinoxes and solstices begin on the same day each year, therefore the zodiac (Sun) signs and their dates do not change.

In terms of mental gymnastics, I'm gonna need you to do a back handspring now. Let's start with some light stretching. The Moon, commonly referred to as a *satellite,* orbits the Earth. This is the closest body to our planet. In the twelve months of our year, there are *twelve (sometimes thirteen, in the case of Blue Moons)* lunar cycles. By lunar cycle, I am referring to the process of the moon beginning "new" (or falling in front of the Sun, invisible due to blocking the light rays), waxing, becoming "full", and waning back down to "new".

This whole process takes approximately 29.5 days. Due to the moon making its merry way around the Earth, you will always find its position within one of the zodiacal constellations. The point I want you to note, *the Moon changes sign every two to three days.* Unless you were born on a new moon, you *will not* have the same Sun sign as your moon sign. While not hugely important, this

Simplified Astrology - 59

connection is missed in much beginner astrology literature. The inverse is true as well, you will only find a full moon when the Sun and moon are in direct opposition of each other (180° angle).

When we expand on the natures of the moon, you will likely relate to your moon sign even more than your Sun sign. This theme is extrapolated throughout our solar system. You will have a sign for each planet in the solar system, relative to their location at the time of your birth. Through obtaining your accurate chart, you will identify with all of these elements, albeit in different areas of the self. Correspondence cannot be overstated. The qualities, sizes, colors, and orbits all indicate *which* part of the self each planet corresponds with.

As we will discuss, even the *glyphs* representing the planets were created methodically in correspondence with the energy of the planet. These pictures are worth thousands of words.

Simplified Astrology - 60

The Sun

As we owe *quite literally everything* to the Sun, we have to start here. The Earth's relationship to the Sun is a beautiful one. All life on our planet is sustained through the energy of the Sun. This star is the same reason we can even *see* the planet we're living on. It is the movement of the Earth around the Sun which allows us to measure our days, weeks, months, and even years. The Sun is our measure for time, which allows us to clock the speed of the other planets.

Without a doubt, the Sun is the most important part of the natal chart. In regards to *the self,* this is the biggest and brightest part of you. Simply put, this is the part we see. Filtered through the energy of its zodiac sign, the Sun shows your conscious awareness and the actions you take. The modus operandi of the Sun is to express itself and fulfill the ego (be seen and felt). Expressions of the will are expressions of the Sun sign. One may easily identify with (and be identified as) their Sun sign, as this is the driving force in all of our lives. For example, if you were born under the sign of Gemini, your *conscious awareness* and *conscious actions*

Simplified Astrology - 61

are those of a Gemini. If that sounds watered down or *vague,* it's supposed to be. We haven't even plugged in the rest of the planets or looked at those angles yet.

I want to bring your attention to the shape of the glyph representing the Sun. We have a point within a perfect circle. In this way, the Sun is marked physically as the center of our solar system. All other bodies in the solar system orbit around this one body. At its core, the Sun represents the center of who you are. This is the same reason the *solar plexus* is the center of the human body. Circles, or parts of circles, are consistently used in astrological glyphs. Circles are used to represent the infinite cycle of life, death, and rebirth as there is no beginning or end to the shape.

Simplified Astrology - 62

The Moon

There are whole libraries of books written about the moon alone. Due to its proximity, the moon illuminates our night sky and controls the tides of our oceans. As the majority of our physical bodies are also water, we can notice the moon's energetic influence *through our bodies.* Whether we are aware of it or not, the moon is something *all of us* feel. Statistics show an increase of 911 calls, hospital admissions, violent crimes and even car crashes when the moon is full. With this pattern continuing perpetually, it is hard for skeptics to claim correlation doesn't equal causation.

Given the moons orbit *inside* the circumference of Earth, rather than the circumference of the Sun, we conclude the moon is our *inner self.* This luminary exposes who we are internally, or in the immediately *unseen* aspects of ourselves. The reflection of our conscious awareness brings us into our feminine natures through the subconscious. The word *feminine* is used to represent *receptivity,* and not gender or sex. This is in direct opposition of the "masculine" or *expressive* natures of the Sun. During the day,

Simplified Astrology - 63

when the Sun is at play, you will rarely see the moon. During the night, you can either use your conscious awareness to look at the moon in the sky, or you can bring your awareness within your other bodies and travel to other levels of your consciousness (also known as dreaming).

Your *feelings* (when not deliberating expressing your will) and *reactions* to what you feel are the realm of your moon sign. Again, this is your *internal* self. You will find yourself in your moon signs energy in your day-to-day life, especially activities which do not require all of your conscious awareness or intentional action. Your internal tides, caused by your moon's rhythm, will urge you to find a sense of emotional stability, balance, or equilibrium in your everyday events. The desire of the moon is to *be comfortable.* This desire manifests itself in many different ways according to the zodiac.

With the moon moving so fast around the zodiac wheel, this is a very important body to watch as you study astrology. If you check the weather daily, check the moon sign as well. If you are a beginner, I would go as far as to say this is the *most important* body for you to watch. As mentioned previously, the moon changes sign every two to three days, allowing you to get a different energy that you can *feel physically inside of your body.*

Simplified Astrology - 64

Connecting these energies with your body is an integral part of the process which is *using this information so you won't lose it.*

I am well aware this does not warrant an explanation; the Moon's glyph is based on the crescent shape *of the Moon.* Given the various phases, the Moon exhibits a crescent shape most of the time. You've seen the Moon, right?

Simplified Astrology - 65

Mercury

While only slightly bigger than our moon, this red hot planet sits closest to the Sun and completes its orbit in a short 88 days. Except in periods of retrograde, you can't expect Mercury to stay in one place very long. With this body sitting so close to the Sun (the brightest part of you), special focus must be placed here as well in regards to the self. Mercury (natally or otherwise) indicates elements of the *mind* or *intellect*.

The attributions and names of the planets based on various gods have been passed down from pantheon to pantheon; however the narrative has remained unchanged. In all stories, from Sumerian to Roman, Mercury acted as a messenger of the gods. Usually equipped with winged-feet or some other flying equivalent, this god was able to freely travel between the physical and spiritual world to convey information or act as a guide. The transfer of information is the key underlying theme. Given its

Simplified Astrology - 66

proximity to the Sun, our biggest source of *information*, this only makes sense.

Within your chart, your natal Mercury indicates the manner in which you *think* and *speak*. The placements and aspects here will also influence *how you communicate* and *how your voice sounds*. Due to the quick-moving pace, this is another body which gives good returns on the attention you pay to it (especially when viewed in relation to your natal Mercury). In transit, Mercury affects the collective mode of thought. A distinction must be made here, Mercury affects *logical* thought (the left hemisphere of the brain) rather than intuition. The quick-moving planet's nature is that of rationality and "square" thinking.

Interestingly, Mercury regularly enters retrograde periods each year. "Retrograde" is a term to describe the optical illusion of a planet appearing to move backwards due to the Earth's perspective of the elliptical transit. Mercury is not the only planet that does this. During retrograde periods, the energy the planet expresses is slowed down, halted, and sometimes even reversed. Not only do retrogrades extend the amount of time in which a planet stays under a sign, elements of the past resurface as *cause and effect* has time to catch up with us.

Simplified Astrology - 67

During periods of Mercury retrograde, which can last nearly a month, past thoughts come to revisit and one will inevitably find themselves retrospecting. In these times, travel and communication may be more difficult than usual as *the intellect (and everything built out of the intellect)* is slowed down on a collective level. These times are usually marked with miscommunications (even arguments), being late, internet buffering, and misreads when you swipe your card at the grocery store to name a few things.

As the name suggests, during retrograde periods it is recommended to *retrospect.* Rest and relaxation are paramount parts of integrating the lessons life is trying to teach you. Retrogrades are not to be feared. *Astrology should never limit your personal power.* However "inopportune" retrogrades may be, keep in mind your expectations influence your outcomes. If you treat yourself with grace and expect lessons; information will expand into your life. If you stress yourself out and expect a rough time; trials and tribulation will expand for you. *Choices are yours to make.* Make good choices, my friend.

We should also analyze Mercury's glyph for more information. There are three distinct elements of our picture. You can see these basic shapes repeated in the form of the other planets

Simplified Astrology - 68

as well. On the bottom of Mercury, we see an equal-armed cross (called the Cross of Matter), representing the physicality of the world. The circle sitting atop the cross again represents the infinite nature of life, existing on top of the material. The crescent resting on the top of the glyph indicates the upward reaching influence of *the mind.*

♀

Venus

Next in line, we have Venus. Falling in between the Sun and Earth, Venus represents much for us astrologically. Even though Venus is further away from the Sun than Mercury, it is *the hottest* planet in our solar system. The thick atmosphere of the planet creates a greenhouse effect with the Sun's rays, making the surface over 900°F. It only takes 225 Earth days for Venus to make a complete lap around the Sun. Venus also rotates *backwards,* causing the Sun rise in the west and set in the eastern horizon.

Venus is named after the Roman goddess of love. Love and appreciation are key elements of the energy expressed by Venus (or the mythological equal). In a natal chart, Venus will indicate the manner in which one *loves* or expresses *value* or *appreciation.* The feminine nature of Venus indicates its influence is felt in a subtle, receptive way as opposed to a forceful or expressive modality. Attraction is the keyword. Due to its correspondence with *value,* the energy of Venus also indicates the

Simplified Astrology - 70

flow of money in one's life, as well as what one prefers to spend their money on.

Not only does Venus (through placements and aspects) indicate your amorous natures, it also shows what you may consider *beautiful* or *valuable*. Your values reveal themselves through the people, places, and things you are willing to compromise with. For this reason, it is very important to be mindful of Venus placements in romantic relationships. We will discuss later on, Venus is very important for synastry in terms of *attraction*.

You probably noticed the glyph for Venus is almost identical to the glyph of Mercury, minus the crescent. Again, we have the circle of life, resting atop the cross of matter. The glyph symbolizes the spirit of life dominating the physical world. In this way, Venus represents a force of attraction or generation.

Mars

Apart from our own planet, Mars is one of the most explored bodies in our solar system. Mars is the fourth planet from the Sun, Earth being the third. Mars completes its revolution around the Sun in 687 days (one Martian year). The surface of Mars contains iron minerals. Due to oxidation, rust is created giving Mars its bright red color. I believe this is why ceremonial magicians attribute iron as "the metal of Mars".

Mars is widely thought to be the "opposite" of Venus. A polarity *does* exist, but they are not opposites. However, the opposing elements worth noting are: the two spin in different directions and Mars offers a masculine (expressive) energy while Venus exhibits a feminine (receptive) one. Color theory also indicates the energy the planets give off, as colors are just *different frequencies* of light.

In the case of Mars, the bright red color indicates *virility, passion, and action.* Mythologically, Mars is the Roman god of war. War-like associations to this planet have existed since the Babylonian times (read about Nergal if you're interested). In a natal chart, Mars indicates expressive *energy.* Your aggressive and masculine natures are expressed through Mars. The nature of Mars is to *take action* aligned with *desire.*

The aspects of your Mars will shed light into your tendencies to be *ambitious, impulsive, or even violent.* Are there any kids still in the room? Let's talk about sex! Sex is a textbook example of desire-driven action. For this reason, Mars is another high-focus planet in synastry charts as it can indicate sexual chemistry (or a lack of one) and elements of conflict. In non-romantic relationships, the elements of Mars are still important. The aspects of Mars can make the difference between garnering your friend's support of your ambitions and starting a fight with that same friend.

Mars is represented symbolically as a circle with an arrow protruding from the upper-right edge. The life giving circle represents energy being directed through the arrow, upward and outward. The direction of the arrow corresponds to the right arm and right hand, which is the driving force for most people. Some see a shield and a spear within the glyph of Mars, which also connects it to its warlike associations.

Simplified Astrology - 73

♃

Jupiter

I find this is an appropriate time to mention (if you haven't noticed already), the further away we get from the Sun, the longer it takes for the planets to complete their orbit. When we approach the slower planets, especially the ones on the outside of the solar system, we have to acknowledge that the influences are stretched across a wider spectrum. Quite literally, the energy covers more space before it reaches the Earth. Due to slower moving planets staying within zodiac signs longer, the effects on the individual may be seen *generationally,* rather than *personally.*

In the case of Jupiter, we are still close enough to be seen with the naked eye. It takes approximately twelve years (4,333 days) for Jupiter to make it around the Sun. Changing signs roughly each year, Jupiter's effects are inconsistent throughout each generation. Without a doubt, Jupiter is the largest planet in the solar system. Compared to the Earth, we're looking at a grape *versus a basketball.* The vast majority of Jupiter's mass is

Simplified Astrology - 74

composed of various gasses. Astronomers estimate if Jupiter even has a solid core, it is quite small in proportion to the amount of gas.

The role Jupiter plays across all stories is *king of the gods,* which we can likely attribute this to the massive size. Jupiterian energy carries the theme of *benevolence, wisdom, faith, and expansion* (as any god-king should) throughout the mythos. Astrologers long ago assigned the title of "Greater Benefic" to this planet, as the effects on humanity are at large, positive.

In practice, your natal Jupiter gives information on your philosophies as well as ethical and moral standards. Here we also find your interests in higher education, religious beliefs, and even the manner in which you share what has been given to you. Continuing the theme of *expansiveness,* Jupiter's position within a chart can indicate in which areas one may find benefits, such as financial/material gains or advantageous opportunities. In this same area of life, things are done on a large scale.

The symbol of Jupiter is an equal armed cross with a crescent attached to the left arm. The crescent, facing outwards, places emphasis on expansion and growth, rather than contraction or stagnation.

Simplified Astrology - 75

♄

Saturn

Far out, man! This is the last planet we can physically see with the naked eye. Saturn's orbit around the Sun takes roughly 29.5 years (that's 10,759 Earth days)! We can expect Saturn to stay under a sign for roughly two and a half years. Just like Jupiter, Saturn is composed mostly of gas and has a system of rings around its body. Including the luminaries, Saturn is the seventh body in our astrological equation.

According to the Romans, Saturn is the father of Jupiter (as well as Neptune & Pluto). In the Greek pantheon, which Saturn is derived from, Kronos is the *god of time*. Legend has it, Kronos (or Saturn) was satiated by eating his own children as Gaia, his mother, warned him that he would be overthrown by his offspring. In this way he was able to sustain himself, as well as avoid being usurped in his position by his family. According to the story, Zeus (Jupiter) eventually defeated his father with force and banished him from the sky he once ruled.

Simplified Astrology - 76

Mythology, mysticism, science, and religion are elements which are mysteriously blended together with many layers. The abridged story of Kronos captures the essence of Saturn's energy quite well. Time rules over the material world. We see this demonstrated as new life replaces old life. Saturn is *formation* and *structure.* Through transit, Saturn shows us the value of hard work and diligence required to maintain our status.

Astrologers refer to Saturn as the "Greater Malefic" first due to its size, and second due to the rigidity of the lessons it comes with. Saturn represents *limitations,* and things which cannot be changed (such as time). Through the energy of Saturn, we learn where the *restrictions* and *boundaries* are in our world. As unrelenting as it seems, Saturn can also be your best friend. It is the nature of the stellar intelligences to assist us in our growth. Saturn assists us through tough love. Through trial and error, we learn about the hard work and solid foundations required to build our Tower. Missing either element inevitably brings our Tower crashing back down to Earth.

Saturnian influence comes in cycles. One may be completely unaware of the effect Saturn has on them until the planet creates a prominent aspect with *their natal Saturn,* as in the Saturn Return. Somewhere between the ages of 27-30, Saturn will

Simplified Astrology - 77

find itself in the same sign and degree as it was when you were born (this marks the beginning of *your* Saturn return). Entirely dependent on the choices you make in your life, this can be a pleasant time *or a terrible one.* The responsible ones who make a note of the Saturnian lessons breeze through these periods relatively unscathed. For many, the late-twenties can be marked as a difficult time of change or collapse. At this age, many people experience a forced change of career, divorce, or their *first midlife crisis.*

The symbol of Saturn is represented as an equal-armed cross with a crescent shape protruding from the bottom. In this way, we see the cross of matter dominating *time*, as indicated by the crescent shape (corresponding to the ebbs and flows of the Moon). Almost directly opposite the glyph of Jupiter, Saturn is shown as a force of structure and limitation, rather than expansion and growth.

Simplified Astrology - 78

Uranus

It is widely accepted that Uranus marks the beginning of the "outer planets". Uranus was the first planet to be discovered by telescope, by astronomer William Herschel. Interestingly enough, the original name for Uranus was George (or Georgium Sidus, after King George III). The name obviously didn't stick as astrologers opted to continue using the Roman pantheon and the corresponding mythos.

Physically, Uranus is a *strange* planet. Not only is Uranus about 20 astronomical units away from the Sun (that's the length between the Sun and the Earth, times twenty), it's clearly *different*. Just like Venus, we see Uranus spinning opposite the rest of the other planets. What's even weirder about Uranus, the axis on which it rotates, *is titled on its side.* Noncompliant, to say the least. Astronomers speculate the unorthodox angle of Uranus is due to the gravitational forces of the surrounding planets, and not the result of a past collision. These gravitational forces are also thought to be the reason for the vertical alignment of Uranus' rings and moon orbits.

With so much distance between Curious George and the center of our solar system, it takes Uranus just over 84 years to complete its revolution. While not everyone gets to experience their Uranus Return, most of us will feel the energy of the other major aspects, such as the first Uranus square (at 21) and the Uranus Opposition (age 42). In the western world, these ages represent adulthood, and your *second midlife crisis* (respectively). Those *not* in crisis mode may experience a *kundalini awakening* or another huge energetic shift in their early forties (for better or worse).

The discovery of Uranus was monumental for astrologers. Finding correspondence for twelve zodiac signs using only *seven* planetary bodies proved to be somewhat limiting. Astrologers were forced to conclude planetary *rulership* stretched over multiple signs (such as Mercury ruling Gemini & Virgo or Jupiter in the case of Sagittarius & Pisces). The discovery of new planets filled in many of the blanks for astrologers and drew new connections about the model we were previously working with.

While we won't cover planetary rulership until *after* the planets, we can discuss polarity. The addition of the outer planets

Simplified Astrology - 80

brought about new ways of looking at the inner ones. With Uranus, the connections to Mercury are undeniable. Uranus is the *higher octave of Mercury* and Mercury is the *lower octave of Uranus*. Although sometimes unpredictable in transit, Uranus affects *massive change* individually as well as collectively. In fact, the historical influences are sometimes easier to spot on account of the planet moving so slowly across the zodiac.

Extending from Mercury, Uranian influence is that of *the mind*. The vastly bigger size of Uranus and it's inherently unique characteristics connect us with *higher levels* of consciousness and our sense of *freedom* or *individuality*. Uranus assists us with making change necessary to align with our higher goals and dreams. Our natal Uranus can indicate the manner in which we think, more importantly how we individualize ourselves mentally. Uranus also shows the friends we make and groups we choose to be a part of, as these align with our mentality.

Given that Uranus stays under a sign for seven years, house position and aspects are key for determining how influence is felt for those of a similar age.

Simplified Astrology - 81

♆

Neptune

In 1846, only 65 years after the discovery of Uranus, the planet Neptune was discovered 30 astronomical units away from the Sun through mathematical calculation. Because of this vast distance, Neptune takes approximately 164 years to transit the zodiac, therefore spending roughly 13 years under each sign. We can deduce the significance of Neptune is largely generational rather than personal. Also, good luck making it to your Neptune Return, bud.

Continuing in chronological order, we find Neptune to be the *higher octave of Venus,* and Venus to be the *lower octave of Neptune.* As in the case of Venus, we also find Neptune to be a generative force but on a broader spectrum (indicated from the mass being over five times bigger). Neptune's influence is spiritual or imaginative in nature, contrasting Venus' reach through physical and emotional elements. These elements create an archetype of *spiritual expansion.*

Neptune in the natal context indicates the creative and imaginative faculties of the individual when viewed through house

Simplified Astrology - 82

and aspect. Generationally, or through the signs, individuals sharing the same Neptune placement may share spiritual priorities or similar "destinies". Due to the subtler cognitive effects of Neptunian energy, Neptune in transit can either be mystifying or enlightening with its influence. Choice and *discernment* are the deciding factors between *truth* and *illusion* when it comes to the images Neptune stirs up in the individual.

Simplified Astrology - 83

Pluto

Since its discovery in 1930, Pluto has undergone many changes of classification. Pluto is even smaller than our Moon, and given its position 39 astronomical units away from the Sun many questions have arisen from this body. Is it a planet? Does it even belong in our solar system? *Currently,* Pluto is classified as a *dwarf planet. Technically,* it is a planet. However huge (and mysteriously oblong) the orbit of Pluto is, the path is clearly around the Sun. Pluto's revolution of the zodiac is over 248 years! That's 20 to 30 years per sign! The variance in time is caused by the eccentric orbit.

As with the other outer planets through the signs of the zodiac, Pluto's influence is of generational and historical significance. House placement and aspects in your natal chart will indicate this planet's individual influence on you (same with every planet). Again following the sequence, we conclude Pluto is the *higher octave of Mars,* and Mars is the *lower octave of Pluto.*

Simplified Astrology - 84

The effect of Pluto is *transformation*. As is usually seen through our *actions,* desire is the prerequisite for change. The powers of Pluto can be either regenerative or destructive. In transit Pluto creates *irreversible change,* usually in the area of the corresponding sign. A prime example is the Pluto-Saturn conjunction in the sign of Capricorn in January of 2020, ringing in the start of a global pandemic (transforming health & structure). Bear in mind, *death is also transformation.* This is no reason to fear Pluto, however. On a personal level, we see Plutonian influence indicates *what areas of life* or in *what ways* we regenerate ourselves.

The physical obscurity of Pluto gives many clues to its energetic natures. The slow movement and monumental distance from the Earth shows that Plutonian energy affects us on a *mass level*, and *in areas we are not always consciously aware of.* When viewed individually (through house and aspect), Pluto also shows how the subtle faculties of the mind are used. Here we can find one's dispositions to spirituality, the occult, magick, and even violence.

Simplified Astrology

⚷

Chiron

With its discovery in 1977, Chiron changed (yet again) the previous astrological model we were working with. Over time, Chiron connected many dots for us given extensive research and observation. Chiron is technically not a planet or an asteroid. It displays many comet-like qualities. As always, physical correspondence will tell us what we need to know - and mythology will expand the meaning with allegories.

Chiron's orbit passes between Saturn and Uranus and takes roughly fifty years to traverse the zodiac. Technically classified as a *centaur,* this body acts as a bridge between the inner and outer planets. Being aware of and working with the energy of Chiron will assist one in the mastery or refinement of the physical - and lead them into the "higher" aspects of the spirit. This sounds great! Now what's the catch?

The chirotic energy is *hard* and *painful.* Let's dip our toes into the mythology to see what Chiron is about. Legend has it, Chiron is the son of Kronos. One day while in the form of a horse,

Simplified Astrology - 86

Kronos knocked up a nymph (nature spirit). It is implied that Kronos took on the form of a horse to hide said relations from his wife. As a result, Chiron was born with his father nowhere to be found. Upon meeting Chiron, Philyra (the nymph) was horrified by what she saw. His body had taken the form of half-man and half-horse; horse being the bottom half. Philyra was not willing to take care of her child and his strange birth-defects, and thus abandoned him.

By what seemed like a stroke of luck, the god Apollo found Chiron and took care of him as his own. Apollo's relationship to Chiron was that of a father-figure but more specifically a mentor. As the Sun god, Apollo has a complete conscious awareness of what occurs on the planet and thus was able to pour vast amounts of wisdom and information into Chiron. He was taught art, science, mathematics, archery, architecture, chemistry, and healing, just to name a few things.

Throughout much of the corresponding mythos, Chiron became renowned for his wisdom and ability to heal others. Many heroes in the congruent stories were trained by Chiron. There are some slight discrepancies in the narrative depending on who you ask, so I'll give you the ending that fits the astrological model. As a hybrid of man and horse, Chiron and other centaurs possess the

Simplified Astrology - 87

intellect of a man and the instinct of an animal. Regardless of how the story ends, keep in mind the inborn dilemma that one of this kind has.

Given the *divine intervention* that Chiron experienced in his early life, his humanity and intellect was expanded to unnatural levels. However, this did not change the fact that Chiron was a centaur. His problematic conception forced him to inherit trauma and *a literal mutation.* With this mutation, Chiron did not share the same immortality that his father possessed. After a long career of healing and helping others, Chiron was still unable to help himself. The nature of his wounding forbade him from finding peace in his lifetime. Chiron tragically but fearlessly took his own life. And thus, the archetype of *The Wounded Healer* was born.

I believe this story is grim but necessary in order to conceptualize how the Chirotic energy affects one. The influence of Chiron, astrologically speaking, is very similar to *wounding.* The natal position of Chiron can indicate in what areas one feels *the most hurt* or disempowered. Sometimes our physical upbringing or inherited traumas can reflect our natal Chiron. Regardless of sign or house position, Chiron's influence can carry themes of *shame, resentment, guilt, self-sabotage, lack of belonging, etc.*

Simplified Astrology - 88

Every one of us has problems, for those are the rites of passage here on Earth. When we are ready to meet ourselves on a deeper level, Chiron initiates us into the next part of our journey. By paying attention to our deepest wounds and choosing to do better - we connect with *higher* aspects of ourselves. Again, this is the bridge or stepping-stone to the outer planets. When we examine how pain (and pleasure) programs the self on a less-than-conscious level, we gain a larger perspective of the spirit and a greater awareness in our lives.

I do not subscribe to the idea that one's Chiron is *unhealable.* As a belief, this is very harmful and limiting. Given the story and how the energy works, I see why some choose to believe this. Your natal Chiron (through house, sign, and aspect) can indicate an area in which you can innately help others. This can prompt one to wonder why they can't help themselves as effectively in the same area. *Why can't I take my own advice? Is there something wrong with me?*

Chiron effectively initiates one into their "spiritual journey" - and this means something different to literally everybody. In order to begin this journey, a level of shadow work must be done (in the Jungian context of the term). I do not want to label, limit, or heavily influence your expectation when it comes to

Simplified Astrology - 89

this centaur. I wish to make you aware that this energy warrants self-psychoanalysis, emotional honesty, and some pain as well.

I want to circle back to the physical elements of Chiron. Like I stated earlier, it closely resembles a comet as it transits through our solar system. Given the vast distance from the Sun, Chiron has a large, icy tail that follows its orbit. When the Sun's rays hit Chiron, the ice transforms directly into gas - completely skipping the liquid form. We will expand on the energetic qualities of matter very soon, but this phenomenon is extremely significant.

This process mirrors the essence of what healing truly is. The densest material becomes the lightest (and freed from bondage) when conscious awareness and right action is given to it. The message Chiron gives us is that through attention to detail, love, forgiveness, and health - we can transcend almost anything.

Simplified Astrology - 90

☊ ☋

North & South Node

We saved the best for last! These nodes are the furthest thing from a planet, but they offer the most profound insight in a natal chart. The lunar nodes are points in which the Moon intersects the ecliptic in its orbit around the Earth. Wherever this point happens to be, an axis is formed and we can thus predict the next intersection. Every two weeks the Moon will make this point of contact and form a node. Due to the perpendicular intersection of the Moon and the Earth's orbital patterns - the series of nodes move retrograde across the zodiac and stay in a sign for 18 and a half years. Your location on Earth will tell you whether the node is northern or southern - given the direction the Moon is moving.

Almost every astrologer will tell you these nodes are linked to karma. But not all of them will tell you how or why that is. We will cover the lunar cycle in more depth later on - for now I want you to consider the Moon's rhythm and cycles as it observes our

Simplified Astrology - 91

planet. Whether you see the Moon as a sentient being or not really doesn't matter when you consider the energies it picks up from *its surroundings*. The patterns of the stars in the zodiac wheel (and every constellation) are being directed straight towards the Moon (and every planet). When we observe the Earth's line of sight to any of the planetary bodies or imaginary points - there will be a constellation behind it indicating what energy it expresses to us.

The lunar cycle is a very effective way to measure time, as the Moon is our biggest and fastest satellite. Lunar nodes are very significant to the cycle because the Sun is *directly involved*. This is a bridge between the conscious (Sun) and the subconscious (Moon). Effectively, lunar nodes will show us the maximum or minimum potential of what there is to be learned in any given cycle. Moving in the southern direction, we see energy we have already experienced (from the perspective of the ecliptic). In essence, this is why the South node is the source of one's karma. We find the *causes* here. In the northern moving direction, this the energy our planet is collectively moving towards. *The future.* The lessons you need to learn.

Generally speaking, with a working understanding of nodes one will consciously start to pursue the North node. Don't shun or isolate the south one. You will do well to create a balance between

Simplified Astrology - 92

the two, as the South node indicates what you already have great experience or proficiency with. Bearing in mind that you are here to learn, working with your South node may be natural and very easy. However, the results of your effort may prove more and more unrewarding or tiresome. Time naturally steers one towards their metaphysical "north". In your natal chart pay attention to sign, house placement, and aspects created with the North and South nodes.

Karma is created *everywhere & at all times.* The nodes within your chart will help illustrate to you in what ways you have been working with the influence of karma. To know where you are going, *you must know where you've been.*

Simplified Astrology - 93

The Zodiac Signs

We have covered much leading up to this point. When it comes to astrology, correspondence cannot be overstated. Understanding correspondence is actually *necessary* to possess a functional usage of astrology. All of the previously discussed components will find their way into the zodiac signs.

The word "zodiac" comes from Greek with a literal translation of "circle of animals". The patterns of the constellations *loosely* resemble animals. In fact, four of the twelve signs in the belt don't even correspond to animals at all. Even among this slight inconsistency, there is much value and information in the symbols presented by the constellations. You already know what a picture is worth. Pictures of nature help us connect to the *natural world* and *ourselves*.

There are many ways to classify or categorize the signs of the zodiac. I have found the most useful distinctions to be:

1.   Element
2.   Modality
3.   Duplicity
4.   Planetary Rulership
5.   Corresponding House

Simplified Astrology - 94

In regards to ***element,*** this refers to alchemical composition and not placement on the periodic table. The essence of alchemy (the practice from which chemistry is derived) is to break down and then refine materials into their purest forms. The various processes of refinement (such as dissolution, calcination, oxidation, etc) showed alchemists that matter responds differently according to energy (ex. *Observer Effect* and *placebos).* In this context, *element* refers to an energetic component. Largely, the empirical shift of thought has taken us away from the spiritual and energetic aspects of matter. There are four distinct elements which we will look at.

Modality is the modification of an element. Through classification, we are able to see the ways in which the four basic elemental energies manifest. The modes are as easy as 123. There are literally only three modes. The essence of these modes are *generation, order, and decay* (respectively).

Duplicity is the most sophisticated way we can say "polarity" in regards to the zodiac. Each sign has a masculine or feminine quality. Again, this has nothing to do with physical gender. *Expression* or *receptivity* is the root of duplicity. Attraction or repulsion. Positive or negative, if you will.

Simplified Astrology - 95

Planetary Rulership is what ties the astrological components together. "Rulership" is jargon which confuses many. Apart from the physical laws of the universe, it is concluded *there are no rules in space.* The planetary bodies do not possess ownership over *anything really,* just their own energy. Simply put, rulership is *energetic correspondence.* In terms of vibration, "rulership" is assigned to the sign exhibiting the most harmony or resonance with a planet. This concept of rulership also allows us to deduce *exaltation* and *debilitation* (powerful or weak positions).

Corresponding Houses are only to be used as a beginner to assist your memory. I must remind you, it is a crutch. The zodiac signs are inherently different from the astrological houses, in fact they are completely separate components, but this doesn't mean you won't find correspondence. If you choose to use this form of delineation, please keep it organized. First house would correspond to the first sign (Aries), the second with Taurus, third with Gemini and so on.

The Elements

At first, this gymnastic exercise we are about to perform may be a bit tricky. It becomes easier when we understand the purpose for doing it. Through the energetic qualities of the *states of*

Simplified Astrology - 96

matter, we are able to divide and classify the world we live in. Classifying matter in this way allows us to classify aspects of the spirit as well (because physical correspondence).

Your science class should've taught you that *solids, liquids, and gasses* (plasmas too, depending on the textbook) are the distinct states matter can be found in. Matter transforms through these respective states as temperature increases. The four elemental components, also in their respective order, are *earth, water, air, and fire.* These words are chosen intentionally not to represent their physical manifestations, but the energetic qualities. To illustrate, earth refers to matter which is solid, like the Moon! Earth is *all physically solid matter,* elementally speaking. In the case of planets like Neptune and Uranus, water and air (liquid and gas) represent entirely different chemical compositions then they do on planet Earth. Elemental fire, corresponding to the state of matter we know *the least about,* exists in more than just flame (think electricity just to get your mind going).

I can admit I currently do not have the knowledge or experience required to write *Simplified Alchemy,* but we really don't need all of the details. The big picture we need to see in regards to these four components: ***all matter contains all four of the elements.*** Regardless if a subject or object physically exhibits

Simplified Astrology - 97

distinct "earthlike, waterlike, firelike, or airlike" qualities, there is an energetic mixture of all four *in everything.* Even the water you drink has an energetic aspect of fire to it.

I can already feel the skeptics getting ready to tell me I've pulled all of this out of my ass. Truly, I wish I could say that I did. Quite literally, alchemy is the science from which chemistry is derived. The four elements we just covered were found through *mathematical* calculation. For brevity's sake we don't need to go into this here. But if you *must* know, do a quick Youtube or Google search on *the platonic solids* and *sacred geometry.*

These same corresponding shapes helped astronomers discover the outer planets in the solar system. If you wondered earlier how some of the planets were discovered through calculation, that's your answer. *Correspondence* and *math*, more specifically through the use of the platonic solids. This is our key for discovering planets beyond Pluto as well. Currently, technology seems to be the limiting factor. Expect astrology and astronomy to evolve in your lifetime; as it has up until this point.

Fire

We're gonna start with the *lightest* and work our way down. The easiest way to understand the alchemical elements is to view them in relation to the individual. After all, we are learning about ourselves here. As a force, fire *burns and consumes.* Fire is a presence which is *seen* and *felt.* Volatile in nature, fire *transforms* matter but can quickly die out or disperse if not properly maintained. Such is true with humans as well.

One's *fire* is synonymous with *passion, desire, willpower, or drive.* Fire is an avenue in which we can direct our energy to what motivates or inspires us. Your *internal* fire indicates how you *see* and *feel* the world, as well as yourself. This perspective, along with your values, is your driving force in life. Fire is the same force that causes you to want to transform aspects of yourself and the world. As you are a mixture of all four elements, balance is key.

To illustrate this point, let's talk about overindulgence. Through correspondence we can notice *lack* as well. We've all heard the term "fired up", right? What comes to mind when I hear the term is a *spaz*, or person with spastic tendencies. A person with *so much energy* who can't stop moving or talking about what has them feeling so passionate is the human embodiment of fire. There are "negative" manifestations of too much fire as well. Think arguments, violence, spite or jealousy. Misdirected passion, or anger, can be quite destructive.

It would be a pretty cold world without fire. We've all felt drained at some point or experienced not having the drive to do something. Same fire, my friend. The only thing worse than having too much of it, is not having enough. Have you ever wondered why we say things like "getting your spark back" or "warming up" regarding taking action? Language has many clues for us. *Creativity* and *vision* are great keywords for elemental fire.

Air

Apart from fire, air is the *lightest* frequency of the elements, vibrationally speaking. Corresponding to gaseous matter, air demonstrates this physically as well. The energetic of air is that of *the mind*, one of the lightest parts of the self. This is the realm of *intellect*, *rationality*, and direct communication (with self and others). Air (ideas/thoughtforms) is the fuel which fire (desire/passion) needs in order to burn. If you've heard the term "airhead" or met a Gemini, chances are you already understand the air energy. It is the nature of those with heavy amounts of air in their elemental mixture to *think* and *talk* a lot.

I'm well aware many use the term "airhead" to indicate the mind is empty, hollow, or stupid. Realistically, this is the opposite of the essence of air. The brain *is not* the mind. The brain is the body's most important sensory organ. In the case of nonlocal perceptions, near-death and out-of-body experiences, we find our ideas are *not stored in the head.* When this distinction is made, the term can no longer be used in the same context. Elemental air *holds* ideas. A *lack of air indicates a lack of ideas.* Relative to an abundance of (useless) thoughts, *airhead* fits both descriptions.

The element of air is the transfer of information. This information is conveyed in a logical, square manner. In this element we are able to communicate with aspects of ourselves and with others.

Water

Water, as we know, holds the shape of its container. It is water's nature to flow within the boundaries of its environment. This is science class for kids, but an esoteric key when combined with hermetic thought. We know water also *holds* an electric charge as well as a vibration. Here we find the energetic component in which *vibration* is held. In our *descendance of matter,* it has been proven scientifically that ideas (air), namely words, influence the molecular structure of water (Dr. Emoto's experiments).

Water is *emotion*; energy in motion. The frequency at which your water vibrates indicates how you feel at any given moment. The amount of elemental water in your mixture will indicate the *intensity* in which you feel said emotions. Again, we see this physically when the Moon pulls on our internal tides. Have you ever been so sad or angry that you cried? Don't lie to me crybaby. In reality, the human body can process any emotion in excess through crying. Tears of joy and tears of grief are tears nonetheless. Life is all about balance, therefore you can find yourself crying for all kinds of reasons.

Earth

Now for the *densest*. Earth, as indicated by our planet, is structure, physicality, and form. Elemental earth is *the material*, and all things associated. In a human, the material archetype corresponds with our environment, our resources, and how we connect our physical body and five senses to the aforementioned. In our own mixtures, it is earth that grounds us to the world we live in as well as allows us to make sense of the world. The knowledge of physical limitation is necessary to work effectively within our bounds.

Earthiness is akin to *practicality* or logic. In extremes, this energy may be viewed as *dull* or *uninspired*. A lack of earth may be unrealistic, delusional, or "out-of-touch". Balance is key.

Modalities

Now that we have covered our four elements, we can begin to expand on them. In the case of our twelve zodiacal signs and twelve houses, each will be assigned an element. We conclude, the four elements are repeated three times each. *Modalities*, or modes, are modifiers of the elements. We have only three modes. All of our repeated elements will have a different expression due to the modality. These are easy as 1-2-3.

Our first modality is ***cardinal.*** Cardinal's Latin roots mean "serving as a hinge". As in the case of a door, a hinge is *preliminary* and *necessary.* Cardinal's astrological context is that of *creativity, initiation, or generation.* These are the beginning stages.

The second modality is ***fixed.*** *Fixation* is the root of what we're looking at. Preservation, sustainability, and resistance to change is the essence of the fixed modality. Here we find our "middle".

Our third modality is what leads us back to the first. ***Mutable*** refers to the dissolution of an element in preparation of the next cardinal wave. Adaptability, flow, and compromise are themes of *mutability.* This is the "end" of the story.

Simplified Astrology - 104

This pattern of modality follows consistently through our wheel. Modalities are easy to memorize and offer much insight about the signs and houses.

Duplicity

Duplicities are even easier than modalities, on account of there only being two of them. I prefer the terms *plus* or *minus*, but you will most likely hear about these in the context of *masculine* or *feminine*. The essence of these terms indicates whether a force is *expressive* or *receptive* in nature. Gender is another hermetic principle which exists in all life, even *independent of physical gender*. Given the two components, the pattern alternates beginning with masculine.

Simplified Astrology - 105

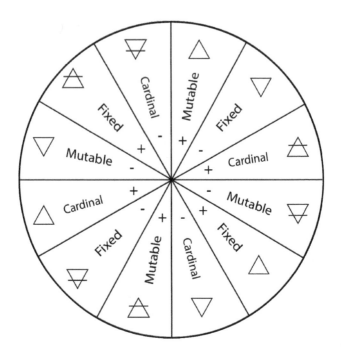

Planetary Rulership

This is an interesting and very important concept in astrology. As mentioned previously, planetary "rulership" has nothing to do with ownership or possession. The term is used metaphorically to describe *resonance* or *energetic harmony* between the planets and signs of the zodiac. The concept of rulership adds four more elements to the equation in regards to our planets. These elements are *home, detriment, exaltation, and fall*.

Simplified Astrology - 106

Half of these are based on polarity so don't worry about memorization. It will come easy.

Home is assigned to the constellation a planet exhibits *the most harmony with.* This is rulership. When we go into the signs next, you will see similarities between the physical aspects of the planets and the zodiac symbols which are considered home. *Detriment* is found by looking at the sign directly opposite a planet's home. Metaphorically speaking, when a planet is in this sign, it is 'away' or 'at work'. *Exaltation* is an elevated or lifted position, different from a planet's home. In this position, the planet has a powerful level of awareness and strong influence. The exalted position is second in power only to a planet's home. The sign opposite a planet's exaltation is where a planet *falls.* A planet in fall is in its weakest or most debilitated state.

The awareness of debilitation can scare beginners when trying to understand their charts. When we move forward, do not be alarmed if some of your planets are in fall or detriment. These placements are not indications of bad fortune, loss, or limitation (but they can be if that's what you make them up in your mind to be). At worst, these are aspects of yourself which require more of your time and attention to grow and develop. As someone with fallen placements, I assure you it's not that bad if you stay out of

Simplified Astrology - 107

your own way. Likely these are balanced with powerful or dignified placements too. The composite of your chart indicates these lessons were the ones you intended to learn in this incarnation in order to expand your awareness spiritually. The contents of your chart do not matter as long as you work it!

It is strongly recommended you draw some form of the chart from the previous page. Using the information you've just acquired will do you a tremendous favor when it comes to retention. Even if you copy the chart verbatim you will have better results. Plus, you'll have a key to refer back to later on. They're your notes, so I won't police them. However you choose to do them: I suggest fill in the blanks as we go. Be sure to check the Tables of Correspondence also, for ease of access. As we cover the zodiac, the dates listed will show when the Sun transits through each sign. This is why your birthday determines your Sun sign.

Aries

March 21 - April 19

Cardinal Fire. Masculine. Home of Mars. First House. I Am.

At the Spring equinox, the ecliptic finds itself touching the cusp of the Aries constellation. The technical term for this is *Right Ascension of the Meridian,* or "ram" for short. To most, this constellation really looks nothing like a ram so if you don't see it, you're not alone. If you've never seen *a real ram*, just know it is the most *appropriately named* animal in the world. A ram will charge head first into almost anything. Charging head first and acting on impulse is the essence of cardinal fire.

Speaking of head first, this brings us to a very important point. Astrologers long ago composed a model of the *melothesic* (zodiacal) man. Each sign in the zodiac wheel was transposed over a part of the human body in order to work with the principle of correspondence. The twelve signs cover your body from head to toe. As the start of our wheel, Aries rules over, or corresponds

Simplified Astrology - 109

with, the head. In theory, you can see the physical constitution of your body in your natal chart. This is an intermediate topic, so I offer it only as food for thought now. The body parts are listed in the Tables of Correspondence if you'd like to give it a go.

As a cardinal sign, the energy of Aries is that of initiation and new beginnings. The bright, red energy of Mars gives Aries natives an air of passion and creative expression. Those born under the sign of Aries or containing heavy Aries energy in their chart may be impulsive in nature. It is the tendency of Arians to take actions quickly and based on desire or emotion. We can also see in the connections to the first house, Aries are direct and sometimes aggressive in expression of *the self.*

It is worth noting, due to the Sun's exaltation in Aries, the more-evolved natives of this sign can exuberate strong self-confidence, willpower, and charisma. Through experience, you will find not all Aries are the same. This is consistent with every Sun sign. We are all *mixtures* of *all of the signs.* As we learn astrology and get a hang of the elements, stay aware we are speaking in "potentials". We're learning about energies *all of us* have access to.

Simplified Astrology - 110

Taurus

April 20 - May 20
Fixed Earth. Feminine. Home of Venus. Second House. I Have.

Next in our wheel of animals, we have the bull. If you, too, enjoy charging headfirst into red flags, you may have Taurus in your chart. That's actually *two* jokes (for the price of one). We all have Taurus in our chart. Some key words for the Taurus energy are *stability, practicality, possession,* and *determination.* As an earth sign, Taurus exhibits a connection to the material and an awareness of *resources.* The influence of Venus can give those born under this sign an appreciation of beauty and material luxuries. This same influence gives Taureans an innate understanding of value.

The fixation on elemental earth is a direct correspondence to the second house. This house is all about our physical and emotional needs, as expressed through *resources* and *values.* Out of a need for physical and emotional security, Taureans are able to pursue their goals to utter completion. When a Taurus identifies

Simplified Astrology - 111

something as valuable, often they will stop at nothing until they possess it. Taurus natives also display possessive or stubborn qualities regarding the things they have. Stubbornness is a consistent quality among all the fixed signs, Taurus expresses this through possessions. Keep in mind: values, morals, and beliefs are things you possess as well. Oftentimes, a Taurus native may be more defensive of their values than their physical possessions. No one really enjoys having their beliefs challenged or dissed. Taureans hate this the most, as their world is centered around logic.

The Moon is exalted in the sign of Taurus. The intention of fixated elemental earth is *stability.* Our Moon sign, as an expression of the subconscious, seeks to be comfortable. This congruence makes Taurus a powerful place for the Moon, natally and in transit. The influence of Venus in this sign also benefits the Moon, as shown in the disposition towards value.

Gemini

May 21 - June 20

Mutable Air. Masculine. Home of Mercury. Third House. I Think.

The constellation of Gemini is said to resemble human twins. I think this is fitting symbolism when viewed in relation to the third house and the element of air. Ideally to communicate your own ideas, you would have at least one other person to talk to. Mutability is also necessary for two people to have a fair conversation and share different ideas within the same environment. In fact, it is this adaptable mental nature of Geminis which gives them their reputation for having "multiple personalities".

It is the rapid pace of Mercury that gives Gemini natives an intellectual *swiftness*. The air element leads these individuals to divide and classify information at a rather rapid pace. Most Geminis become rather skilled at expressing their ideas through language. Words may be used as anchor points to hold onto thoughtforms as the Gemini mind races from one mutable air current to another. Due to their speaking prowess, one may find Geminis are easy to talk to, or at least *relate to* mentally. The Mercurial pace is also the drawback of Gemini, as they are known for monologue or long, drawn out stories.

Physically, Gemini rules over the arms, lungs, and nerves. As this is our first "dual" sign, it only makes sense. Gemini's practical awareness of the subtle nerves as well as the arms and hands (our most useful tools) makes these natives proponents of busyness. These individuals are happiest when given something to do or when entertained with intellectual stimuli. For these people, boredom can come with a sense of despondency.

The tendency to remain mentally stimulated often shapes Geminis into eccentric people. Quick to learn, these individuals have no problem synthesizing or inventing new ideas based on their interests. At large, Geminis are nonconformists. Geminis are easily able to recognize their own uniquenesses and differences. Assisted by their social aptitudes, others easily recognize their individuality as well.

Cancer

June 21 - July 22

Cardinal Water. Feminine. Home of The Moon. Fourth House. I Feel.

Keywords here are *sensitive, intuitive, domesticated,* and *tenacious.* Cancer is appropriately symbolized by the crab, with a tough exterior shell and soft center. Largely, crabs are defensive in nature as they have many natural predators. Crabs are known to work together in order to provide food or protection for their family. Female crabs deliberately search for a comfortable and safe location to release their eggs. Safety and security is of utmost importance for all crabs. Such is life for those born under the sign of Cancer, metaphorically speaking.

Cardinal water comes with an innate perception of *vibration.* As the Moon rules over Cancer, psychic information and messages from the subconscious are normal to the natives of this sign. It is this emotional sensitivity that guides Cancer throughout life, as they are able to intuit danger, be it physical or emotional. Just as a hard shell acts as armor, many Cancers hide shyness or vulnerabilities beneath the surface. Broadly speaking, Cancers do not do well with ridicule or harsh judgements due to their sensitivity. *Caring* is the superpower of Cancer, but also the detriment.

Among friends and family, Cancers express a deep compassion unlike any other. The connections to the fourth house are undeniable as those influenced by Cancer demonstrate a "maternal" type of love to the ones close to them. Just as the Moon has various phases, so do the moods of Cancer. The actions of these individuals may be inconsistent, as they operate largely based on their feelings. While known for having good interests and intentions at heart, it is not uncommon for Cancers to have emotional outbursts, act aggressively, and come at people sideways (pun intended). When comfortable or stable in the emotional realm, the actions Cancers take are *direct* and easily compliant with others. While upset, their actions may become sporadic and the Cancer may self-isolate to relocate equilibrium. Neptune's exaltation in the sign of Cancer is indicated by the strong psychic and imaginative faculties of those born under this sign.

Simplified Astrology - 116

Leo

July 23 - August 22
Fixed Fire. Masculine. Home of The Sun. Fifth House. I Will.

Next we have *The King (or Queen) of the Jungle.* The lion stands proudly as a symbol of *power, pride,* and *nobility.* The Sun's rulership over Leo instills the same radiant, warm qualities in its natives. It is the duty of the Sun to give life, light, and warmth to the solar system, while acting as the center of all activity. The Sun gives freely and generously. In this way Leos may be bold, indiscriminate, and compassionate in how they take action. Leos love to receive attention, or better yet, *be the center of attention.* Any Leo who says they don't enjoy attention is lying to you.

It is the nature of The Sun and elemental fire to be *seen* and *felt.* Leos desire to be seen and felt as well. They choose to be recognized through their actions or their creations. As the fifth house shows us, our creations can be our ideas or even our children. Just like an actual lion, a Leo can be a real threat to you if you mess with their kids. A Leo will also defend their *brainchildren* to the death, as they are very proud and stubborn due to their fixed elements.

Leos develop a keen self-awareness due to the effects they have on others. For those born under this sign, the favor of others (as well as the self) is sought after. Through careful observation, Leos will modify their behavior in order to be held in a higher esteem. Both Leo men and women carry a sense of regality with every action. When the efforts of the will yield power, Leos are generous and bold in their aid of those around them.

Jupiter finds exaltation in the sign of Leo. Both Jupiter and Leo share a theme of expansiveness and benevolence in their influence. The tendency of these individuals to be bold and eccentric fits the narrative of *playing on a large scale.*

Virgo

August 23 - September 22
Mutable Earth. Feminine. Home of Mercury & Chiron.
Sixth House. I Analyze.

Virgo is the second sign of the zodiac not represented with an animal. This is the *virgin woman*. Kinda makes you wonder how they knew that about her just by looking at the stars, but I digress. The corresponding mythology associates Virgo with fertility and harvest. Like a fertile but empty field, mutable earth is ready for any seed you give it.

Key elements of Virgo are *precise analysis, attention to detail,* and *service*. As all earth signs do, Virgos assign importance to logic and hard work. It is Virgos practical awareness and understanding of *process* which gives the natives a disposition towards "perfection". Given the lack of technology and thus planets, Mercury was long ago assigned the rulership of Virgo as well as Gemini. We are able to find correspondence with Mercury

Simplified Astrology - 119

in the intellectual sharpness of Virgo natives, however there is an emphasis on exactness here.

Since the discovery of Chiron, astrologers have poised and tested many theories regarding its rulership. Along with many others, I am inclined to agree Chiron is the ruler of Virgo. Chiron is our bridge between the inner and the outer planets as it passes between Saturn and Uranus. It is through the dichotomy of the sixth and twelfth houses in which the refinement of the physical leads us into the spiritual.

Virgo's connection to the sixth house places emphasis on service and health. Virgos feel most fulfilled when helping others or being *of use.* It is worth noting, Virgo rules over the bowels. When at unrest mentally, Virgos tend to experience stomach issues and a plethora of other illnesses. Mentally disciplined Virgos often find themselves in great health and possess a great resilience towards disease.

Libra

September 23 - October 22
Cardinal Air. Masculine. Home of Venus.
Seventh House. I Balance.

Again, not an animal: we have the constellation of Libra symbolized by *the scales*. Directly opposite Aries and the energy of the first house, we have *relationships*. Traditional scales *require* two objects in order to establish relation, or weight and then find *balance*. This, along with a propensity towards beauty, is the essence of Libra. Those born under this sign have a natural understanding of relationships and self-awareness when around others. The influence of Venus gives Libras a special charm and radiance in the way they carry themselves.

The natives of this sign oftentimes display a need for companionship, be it romantic or otherwise. As an air sign, the relationships Libras form are usually formed on an intellectual connection. Saturn is exalted in this sign, as it expresses a higher understanding of structure and form. It is Saturn's presence that

Simplified Astrology - 121

gives Libras a keen sense of justice and good judgement in relationships. For this same reason, Libras are very vocal when they witness injustice of any sort. Their ability to relate to *anybody* makes Libras especially compassionate to those not as fortunate as them.

Libras thrive on harmony. When those around them are happy, Libras find peace. Confrontations can be an internal dilemma between keeping the peace and being honest and upfront. Although sometimes willing to compromise and give second chances, Libras do not tolerate being treated unfairly.

Scorpio

October 23 - November 21
Fixed Water. Feminine. Home of Pluto & Mars.
Eighth House. I Desire.

Given that scorpions are arachnids, we can see the direct connection to the eighth house. This is also indicated by Pluto's resonance with this sign. The natives of Scorpio have an intensity within their aura, as they are driven strongly by desire to create transformation. Just like all water signs, Scorpios possess innate psychic gifts and keen perception. With it's sextile position to Virgo and the sixth house, Scorpios pay close attention to detail.

The fixation on emotions and mystical influences of the eighth house gives Scorpios an air of mystery and obscurity. As a mechanism for staying emotionally untouchable, Scorpios oftentimes will choose to keep their thoughts and desires secret until they have a general consensus of the emotions of those around them. Like all fixed signs, when a Scorpio decides they want something, they will usually stop at nothing to attain it. With connections to the sexual organs, a Scorpio's desires carry a primal intensity. Romantic relationships involving Scorpios can be deeply passionate and emotional.

The planet Uranus experiences exaltation in the sign of Scorpio. With its strong individuality and tendency to effect changes and revolution, the two make a great pair. Again, it is Uranus which activates the subtle bodies and higher facets of the mind. It is Scorpio's burning desire combined with Uranian insight which prevents them from remaining separated from their goals. Polarity tells us this is the sign of Venus's detriment. Pluto and the eighth house both represent many things which are not considered beautiful, yet are still quite necessary.

Simplified Astrology - 124

Sagittarius

November 22 - December 21
Mutable Fire. Masculine. Home of Jupiter. Ninth House. I See.

The most direct way into the essence of Sagittarius is through the polarity of Gemini and the third house. The extrapolation of interpersonal communication and our immediate environment brings *higher learning* and *wisdom*. Given Jupiter's influence under this sign, expansion and gain is a primary focus for Sagittarius. It is in their nature to live their lives largely and boldly pursue new experiences. The elements of the ninth house often give those born under this sign an evolved or organized set of philosophies and beliefs.

Along with the other fire signs, action and adventure is a must for those influenced by Sagittarius. Set but also adaptable in their ways, Sagittarians know the value of exploration and deliberately pursuing their interests. It is the pole that Gemini and

Sagittarius both rest on which gives them an intellectual acuity and a desire to learn. For Sagittarius, their refined awareness and imagination also enables them to relate to or empathize with *just about anyone.*

With the expansive energy of Sagittarius, the Moon's South Node does well in this position. Many consider this to be the South Nodes sign of exaltation. Through keen analysis and wisdom, we can integrate the lessons of our past and charge valiantly towards our future (North Node). In fact, Karma (Cause and Effect) will repeat the lessons for us time and time again until we really get the message. It is the *wise guy (gal)* with the *wise eye* who can actually see where his karma is coming from, and through intentional action *change it.*

Simplified Astrology - 126

Capricorn

December 21 - January 20
Cardinal Earth. Feminine. Home of Saturn. Tenth House. I Use.

Practical, sturdy, and diligent, Capricorn brings many necessary qualities to our world of form. Through elemental earth and the energy of Saturn, the natives of this sign are born with an ingrained understanding of resources and how through action, structure may be made from them. As the tenth house represents us at our *highest* or maximized potential, the natives of Capricorn often have very clear ideas of what they want and how they are going to get it.

As a cardinal sign, Capricorn diligently takes action and initiates projects according to their goals. Capricorn's practical awareness makes them one of the most *resourceful* signs of the zodiac. Their ability to make use of *almost everything* is the same reason accomplishment seems to come natural to them. It is the

Saturnian influence which instills the drive to work hard and consistently towards better status.

Mars experiences exaltation in the sign of Capricorn. One of the downfalls of Martian energy is *blind passion,* action without clear direction. Cardinal earth assists the planet of personal power to materialize its desires. This position teaches us that with proper planning and structure, our intentional actions will always produce better results. The Moon and Neptune are both weakened in the sign of Capricorn, as emotions and imagination are generally not its forte.

Aquarius

January 21 - February 18
Fixed Air. Masculine. Home of Uranus. Eleventh House. I Know.

If you've seen what Aquarius symbolizes (the water bearer), you may be wondering why this is an air sign. It's quite simple, actually. We already know *water* corresponds to emotion and *air* represents ideas. The real inclination is that through *emotional intelligence,* we can "bear our water". If we deliberately keep our cup full, we can pour it out for others. This is the essence of what Aquarius represents energetically.

The influence of Uranus connects Aquarians to their individuality. Independence and originality are of utmost importance. As air signs, Aquarius natives live their lives intellectually and form relationships on a mental level. Their fixed qualities allow them to remain centered in their mind among most people or ideas. These same fixed qualities give Aquarians their

Simplified Astrology - 129

stubborn or determined natures. The eccentric minds of Aquarius natives can make them prone to arguments and misunderstandings.

The correspondences of the eleventh house brand Aquarius as the sign of *the Humanitarian.* There is a conscious awareness of the *collective* and also where the self fits inside the group. An inborn empathy exists in Aquarius, as their focus is primarily centered on collective benefit. Combined with their mental fixation, Aquarius natives are hard working and loyal to those who share similar ideals and values.

Mercury is exalted in the sign of Aquarius. Communication and logical use of the intellect is actually *necessary* for *any group* to cooperate. For this reason, Mercury does quite well here. For the Sun, this is the sign of its detriment as the true Will of Aquarius is anything but self-centered.

Pisces

February 19 - March 20
Mutable Water. Feminine. Home of Neptune.
Twelfth House. I Believe.

Mystifying only begins to describe what this energy is. As a rule, water signs are gifted with an emotional sensitivity. Prior to the discovery of Neptune, Jupiter was thought to rule over Pisces. Jupiter retains "co-rulership" but Neptune exhibits the most harmony with this sign. Pisceans have strong imaginative faculties and are very receptive to the vibrations around them. The expansive minds of Pisces natives can unconsciously take on the qualities of their environment and the people within.

Due to their keen ability to feel, Pisces understand or at the very least *sense* the emotional worlds of others, and are thus compassionate in their actions. Pisces rules over the feet, which are quite literally required to understand man, as they *stand under*. Mutability is necessary for Pisces to weather the emotional storms of their lives, self-inflicted or otherwise. The symbol for Pisces shows two fish swimming in opposite directions. This is *emotional conflict.*

Pisces also rules the lymphatic system and the liver. The lymphatic system and the liver are both responsible for cleansing the body and regulating our immunity. While usually adept at processing their emotions, Pisces may become physically ill when under duress. Any human, regardless of star sign can become physically ill from emotional blockage, but Pisces are more susceptible due to their sensitivity.

The Neptunian directions Pisces receive keep them hovering *just above* the physical world. Due to the twelfth house correspondence, Pisces see the world through the lens of their imagination and often need to be alone. In solitude, Pisces are able to find peace in their internal waters and find more *clarity* in the conscious. Through the subconscious in particular, Pisces are prone to psychic insight *and* self-deception.

Pisces do well to connect with the *Virgo side* of the axis they sit on. While Neptune can be illuminating, it can be *blinding* also. Self-care and physical refinement of the body and habits can assist Pisces with issues of escapism, depression, or addiction that they may struggle with. Mutable earth can help Pisces balance their intuition and imagination with logic and practicality.

Simplified Astrology - 132

Decans or Decanates

You should know by now that no two people of the same Sun sign are going to be exactly alike. Not only are we a complex energetic mixture of *all the planets PLUS the Sun,* precision matters when going across the zodiac. In reality, the Universe is not as rigid as the 2D maps we use for astrology. Vibration moves like fluid throughout the world, it is not as cut and dry as the cusps on a chart.

Given 360° in our circle, each zodiac sign will get 30°. That's 30 different degrees a planet can fall on (with various spaces in between). The specific details *do* matter when we look for accuracy. To illustrate this point, consider the sign of Aries. 0° Aries is adjacent to Pisces, and thus shares some of the same energetic qualities. 29° Aries is much closer to the sign of Taurus, which would give Aries more fixed-earth qualities. There is a gradient scale of energy throughout each sign.

Decans, or decanates are additional divisions of the twelve zodiacal signs used to further define planetary rulership. A decan represents a space of 10°, therefore each sign will have three decans. There are different approaches to decans and therefore different rulers depending on who you ask. I present to you the

Simplified Astrology - 133

most logical way this has been presented to me and how you can calculate these yourself.

The *first* decan corresponds with the *primary ruler* of the sign. Aries, Mars. Taurus, Venus. Gemini, Mercury. Cancer, Moon. Etc. and so on. The *second* decan is sub-ruled by the ruler of the next sign with the same element. Again, using Aries as an example: the next fire sign in sequence is *Leo.* Leo is ruled by the Sun, and therefore the second decan of Aries is sub-ruled by the Sun. The *third* decan is just one step further. We check the remaining sign of the same element for its ruler. For Aries the third decan is sub-ruled by Jupiter, as Jupiter rules over Sagittarius, the last fire sign.

Tables of Correspondence

Decanates

Sign	1st Decan (0°- 10°)	2nd (10°- 20°)	3rd (20°- 30°)
Aries	Mars	Sun	Jupiter
Taurus	Venus	Chiron & Mercury	Saturn
Gemini	Mercury	Venus	Uranus
Cancer	Moon	Pluto & Mars	Neptune
Leo	Sun	Jupiter	Mars
Virgo	Chiron & Mercury	Saturn	Venus
Libra	Venus	Uranus	Mercury
Scorpio	Pluto & Mars	Neptune	Moon
Sagittarius	Jupiter	Mars	Sun
Capricorn	Saturn	Venus	Chiron & Mercury
Aquarius	Uranus	Mercury	Venus
Pisces	Neptune	Moon	Pluto & Mars

Simplified Astrology - 135

Days of the Week

Day	Planetary Ruler
Monday	Moon
Tuesday	Mars
Wednesday	Mercury
Thursday	Jupiter
Friday	Venus
Saturday	Saturn
Sunday	Sun

Planetary Octaves

Lower Octave	Higher Octave
Mercury	Uranus
Venus	Neptune
Mars	Pluto

Simplified Astrology - 136

Planetary Rulership of the Signs

Sign	Ruler	Exaltation	Detriment	Fall
Aries	Mars	Sun	Venus	Saturn
Taurus	Venus	Moon	Mars	Uranus
Gemini	Mercury	North Node	Jupiter	South Node
Cancer	Moon	Neptune	Saturn	Mars
Leo	Sun	Jupiter	Uranus	Mercury
Virgo	Chiron	Mercury	Neptune	Venus
Libra	Venus	Saturn	Mars	Sun
Scorpio	Pluto	Uranus	Venus	Moon
Sagittarius	Jupiter	South Node	Mercury	North Node
Capricorn	Saturn	Mars	Moon	Neptune
Aquarius	Uranus	Mercury	Sun	Jupiter
Pisces	Neptune	Venus	Chiron	Mercury

Simplified Astrology - 137

Pantheons

Planet	Babylonian	Greek	Roman	Archetype
Sun	Shamash	Helios	Sol	Solar gods
Moon	Sin	Selene	Luna	Lunar gods
Mercury	Nebu	Hermes	Mercury	Messengers
Venus	Ishtar	Aphrodite	Venus	Goddess of love/beauty
Mars	Nergal	Ares	Mars	Gods of war
Jupiter	Marduk	Zeus	Jupiter	Patron gods
Saturn	Ninib	Kronos	Saturn	Time/Structure

Simplified Astrology - 138

The Human Body

Sign	Body Parts or Systems
♈	Head, ears, facial features
♉	Neck, throat, vocal cords, thyroid
♊	Arms, hands, fingers, lungs, nervous system
♋	Chest, breasts, pancreas, stomach
♌	Heart, spine
♍	Digestive system, intestines, spleen
♎	Kidneys, endocrine, lumbar region, skin, buttocks
♏	Reproductive system, sexual organs, excretory
♐	Thighs, sciatic nerve, pituitary gland
♑	Knees, skeletal system, teeth, joints
♒	Calves, shins, ankles, circulatory system
♓	Feet, toes, body fat, lymphatic system

Simplified Astrology - 139

Signs of the Zodiac

Symbol	Sign	Element	Modality	Duplicity	Ruler
♈	Aries	Fire	Cardinal	Masculine	Mars
♉	Taurus	Earth	Fixed	Feminine	Venus
♊	Gemini	Air	Mutable	Masculine	Mercury
♋	Cancer	Water	Cardinal	Feminine	Moon
♌	Leo	Fire	Fixed	Masculine	Sun
♍	Virgo	Earth	Mutable	Feminine	Chiron
♎	Libra	Air	Cardinal	Masculine	Venus
♏	Scorpio	Water	Fixed	Feminine	Pluto
♐	Sagittarius	Fire	Mutable	Masculine	Jupiter
♑	Capricorn	Earth	Cardinal	Feminine	Saturn
♒	Aquarius	Air	Fixed	Masculine	Uranus
♓	Pisces	Water	Mutable	Feminine	Neptune

Simplified Astrology - 140

Simplified Astrology - 141

Reading The Chart

Now that we've gone through all of the major elements in the chart, we can start to look at our composite. It is strongly recommended that you begin with *your own* birth chart (know yourself before others), however you could truly use any chart. As you know, there are theoretically an infinite number of charts we could cast. All we need is a specific location and a specific time to draw out a blueprint.

The Information Age and modern technology has lowered the barrier of entry for astrology dramatically. In the past, you actually needed a *physical ephemeris, an atlas, paper, pencils, protractors, a big eraser,* and *a substantial understanding of math and science* to cast a natal chart. This is obviously no longer the case. There are many free calculators that you can use online to get your birth chart. *Do not pay for this service;* unless you want to buy a fancy printout for your wall or something to that effect. I have decided against listing websites or apps in this book as the specifics will change over time. Your phone or computer will give you what you need, just ask the search engine.

Due to this book being *largely foundational,* I have also taken the liberty of *not* labeling, tabling, and limiting each planet's

Simplified Astrology - 142

placement in every sign and house. By the sheer quantity of placements that can occur within a chart, this is not a simple task. Also, if you aren't actively working with your chart yet, memorizing such lists does not prove useful. There are countless websites and books available that do this if you need all the information compiled for you or want more detail on a specific placement. With enough mental stretching and the tables from the last chapter, you could create your own compilation.

A largely undervalued resource is *online forums.* Even Facebook has a "group" setting where you can engage with hundreds of thousands of people who share common interests, for absolutely free. In this method, you can directly ask a group of people what personal experiences they have had with, let's say "Saturn in Gemini, 2nd house". We are collectively drowning in information and resources, so be sure you use some of the things available to you. *Social astrology apps are a thing too,* take advantage!

We discussed this briefly in the beginning or the book; but I will remind you to stress the importance. Self-awareness comes with responsibility so if you know better - *you should do better.* We should always seek first to understand before we judge. Your chart will show you many facets or yourself. If I catch you saying

Simplified Astrology - 143

"is it bad that my *(insert planet)* is in *(sign/house)*?" I might actually slap the shit out of you. This thought process is far too reactive and you should reread the last section of the first chapter. If you don't want to read it again, here's the summary: *make good choices and don't give your power away to astrology.*

So you have your chart - now what? Now we begin (or continue) the ongoing process of self-realization. What you're really looking at when you gaze at your chart is *you.* Through this tool, you will effectively compartmentalize your *self.* This process begins through analyzing the details of the chart and expanding your familiarity with the various components of who you are.

To give you an example, let's say your birthday is May 5th. You've always known you're a Taurus. You can relate to this label, but intuitively you know *there is more to you.* Through obtaining your chart you learn your Sun sign is Taurus, and that's where the label comes from. Your Moon is way across the chart in the sign of Scorpio. All the other planets are scattered about various signs. You can suddenly *see,* there *is* a whole lot more to you.

In the very beginning of this book, we deliberately organized the pieces of the chart into a specific order. We strayed from this order to learn the elements, but we are circling back to it

Simplified Astrology - 144

now that we have the tools. The most concise way to look at *any* placement in a chart is: ***planet, sign, house, aspect, and then pattern*** (in that order). This arrangement is also the dominant way placements are discussed. To help you understand others (and be understood by them), follow this syntax.

Through the information we've covered already, you should have a functional understanding of the planets. These are the bodies of the solar system, and through correspondence, your chart will display them as *aspects of yourself*. These aspects are modified by the sign they occupy. More specifically, the *house* the placement falls inside of will indicate *where* the energy is personally seen in your life. Aspect (which we haven't covered yet), is the geometric relationship between two or more placements. The *composite of aspects* creates patterns, or bigger pictures to look at. The dance of time keeps all of our elements in motion, so we must bear in mind this is an evolving science, and every relationship will inevitably change.

To effectively self-realize with your chart, begin with planet-signs and work your way up. Most of us, interested in astrology or not, know of our Sun sign. The next logical step is to know the other bodies. Start with memorizing your Moon sign and working your way down the planets from inner to outer. Each of

Simplified Astrology - 145

these planetary bodies will fall in a sign, giving them a different mode of expression. The further we get from the Sun, the slower the body moves across the zodiac. This is why we begin with the inner planets. For example your Pluto sign will hardly ever differ from those of your generation, thus making it much harder to see on an individual level.

When you are comfortable or perhaps even bored of the planet-signs, start to add in their house positions. This is where the picture begins to crystallize mentally. Using our previous example, let's say you found out your Sun sign *(Taurus)* is in your *eleventh house.* Knowing that the eleventh is all about the *collective, friends, dreams, and wishes;* you can see how you do not fit perfectly in the traditional molds or stereotypes of Taurus. You will still carry the qualities of fixed earth, such as logic, stubbornness, ambition, etc. (zodiac sign); but through *action* (the Sun) we will see a disposition towards *altruism, friendship, and humanitarian pursuits* (11th).

Many beginners like to start with their *Big Three* signs. This includes the Sun, the Moon and the Ascendant sign. As the driving force in life, the Sun is very easy to identify with. Representing the emotions, subconscious, and reactions to life, the Moon sign in many ways defines us better than our Sun does. The

Simplified Astrology - 146

ascendant sign is the same thing as your *first house.* Granted that this is not an actual planetary body, it still has huge significance on who you are. The first house is easily seen by others, given that it ascends the horizon *first,* and it also shows you where all your other houses will fall. The first house also has the strongest correspondence to our ideas of what "the self" represents.

If you really were born on May 5th, under a full Moon, with the sign of Cancer on the eastern horizon (1st house), your Sun sign is in the eleventh house. Polarity will tell you Scorpio is your Moon sign. Polarity will also tell you that Scorpio is in your *fifth house.* When you start diving into the specifics of the chart, you will want to view *Your Moon* in its relation to Scorpio *and* the fifth house, as two separate but conjoined elements. This is the same for every planet, asteroid, or focal point of your chart. Keep in mind planetary rulership and the four elements and you will always form some sort of connections while analyzing your chart.

When you get the hang of your planets, start adding the aspects *between the planets* to see their relationship. This is what we are going to cover now. I remind you that the information you've been given has been deliberately simplified for many reasons. We are discussing a tool with various purposes, one of which is *enlightenment* (self-realization). By the very nature of the

Simplified Astrology - 147

process; this is work you must do yourself. I couldn't do it for you even if I wanted to. My sole intent is to familiarize you with the tool's many functions so you are confident enough to do the work by yourself.

Aspects

Now we're going to do the math and connect the dots (literally). Not only is this *easy* and *fun,* this is where all the real information is. When we analyze two or more separate elements in a chart, we can examine their relationship. What we are effectively looking for is *cause and effect,* or an indication of how *one part of the self influences another.* With a working understanding of aspects you can better understand yourself, your interpersonal relationships, and how the universe affects your own chart in transit.

Before we begin, it must be stated that there are *no bad aspects* (only bad choices). Every shape has unique qualities and thus a specific use. Just as the planets and asteroids exhibit positions of power or weakness throughout the zodiac, *harmony* will vary depending on aspect.

Consider that you are here to learn. For ages, the esoteric concept of *squaring the circle* and *circling the square* has been

Simplified Astrology - 148

passed around. Everything in life exists with or inside of a circumference (circle). When we examine the various edges of a circle, we can draw connections using straight lines and math (logic). These lines create many different shapes or polygons. Going back to the square, which is considered *quite harsh* in aspect, we have an object that exemplifies logic and form. Our world of circles includes, but ultimately supersedes form. Like a sculptor with a chisel, intention and effort will eventually chip away the rough edges of the square, turning it into a circle. In this way, we are able to make intuitive (circular) connections about elements limited by logic (squares), and vice versa.

As we discussed with rulership, *harsh aspects* are not a death-sentence. In fact, if we had no squares, *we wouldn't learn anything at all.* If you see a discouraging amount of what appear to be rough angles, understand that these are the keys to your growth. The Universe will *never* give you a hand of cards that you cannot play. Remember this as a testament to your strengths if you ever get tired of chipping away at squares.

Simplified Astrology - 149

Conjunction

    A "perfect" conjunction occurs when two planets in a chart share the same exact degree. Theoretically, conjunctions only occur at an aspect of 0° or 360°. This is a great place to start because it leads us into discussing *orbs*. The word *orb* is synonymous with *sphere*. Bearing in mind the planets are spherical and take up a substantial amount of mass, a margin must be allowed when measuring aspects. The closer an aspect is to the "mathematical standard", the stronger the influence will be.

    Astrologers have determined that conjunctions should have orbs of no larger than 10.8°. A margin larger than 10.8° begins to take on qualities of other minor aspects. When two planets are conjunct, the energies are at large *harmonious.* By sharing similar degree, the planets will effectively "work together" as they are operating in the same mode of expression. This aspect is generally positive in transit and in synastry, as there is a lower chance for friction. Due to the lack of friction, conjunctions may not be a source of lessons or challenges. Further defined by the planets creating this aspect, conjunctions may indicate strong *force* or *powers*.

Opposition

As the name suggests, oppositions occur when two elements are placed *opposite* each other in a chart. Geometrically speaking, this angle is 180° and represented by a straight line. For oppositions, an orb of no more than 10° is allowed. Polarity is the key attribute to this aspect. Due to the polarizing nature of oppositions, it is difficult to say whether they are inherently positive or negative on a broad spectrum.

Linguistically speaking, this aspect implies energies which *oppose* each other. In reality, this is not always the case. The Hermetic Principle of Polarity tells us that *opposites are identical, just varying in degree.* For this reason, oppositions may be the source of more similarities than differences. In your own natal chart, or in synastry with others, oppositions may create balance between two poles or a complete disconnect. In every circumstance, opposition indicates that *something is added,* for better or for worse.

As we have mentioned many times already, each position in our circle rests on a pole. The various poles in the astrological chart serve as bridges between the signs and houses. Each sign or house contains the qualities of its opposite. Although oppositions may actually indicate a *conflict of interest*, they are also the most direct route across the wheel and thus contain much information. Among the signs, opposite placements will share *modality* and *duplicity* but differ in *element.*

Square

A square is an equilateral shape with four vertices, each containing 90°. Thus in an astrological chart, any two elements sharing a 90° angle (with an orb of 7.5° or less) are said to have a *square* position to each other. What is interesting and important to

Simplified Astrology - 152

note with right angles is that they will only occur between signs of the same modality. This is where we find our friction.

Consider the sign of Leo and its relation to Scorpio. These signs share the same modality, yet they differ in element and duplicity. Both signs will have a disposition towards *fixation* or *stubbornness*, but express these dispositions quite differently. The bold and outgoing nature of Leo lies perpendicular to the receptive emotionality of Scorpio.

This positioning can be the source of many misunderstandings or arguments in any sign, as this angle represents an abrupt energetic shift. However, like a puzzle piece, squares also serve as necessary connections between different elements. In transit, planets form squares with the placements of your natal chart and this aspect can create tension and discomfort in your life. This aspect inherently comes with an element of confusion, as it aims to connect two seemingly unrelated points. If you are willing to learn, you will love squares. Of all the aspects, squares have the most to teach.

I do not subscribe to the narrative that squares are bad. At worst, they indicate an opportunity to expand into something new. Consider the only thing worse than "having to deal with" squares

Simplified Astrology - 153

is being so comfortable in your trines and sextiles that you allow yourself to become stagnant.

Trine

Similar to the square, I will not suggest that this shape is good or bad. In a chart, a *trine* aspect is indicated by two elements placed 120° apart, with a max orb of 8.3°. The equilateral triangle is a symbol of synergy. In other words, trine placements add up to *more than* the sum of their parts (also for better or worse). Given the harmonious position between the elements, trines have a natural beauty that the other aspects do not. In a mathematical sense, for two planets to share this aspect, they must be in a sign of the same element.

Synthesis and opportunity is the essence of the trine. This sounds mostly good; and it is. In your natal chart, trines may indicate the things in your life that *just come naturally* to you. The activities that required you no effort to be great at may very well be examples of trines. Keep in mind there is a negative aspect of things coming *too easy* also. A well-positioned trine may make things *just easy enough* for you to not have to exert yourself. As a result, you may allow opportunities to pass you by and neglect to improve yourself. There are no bad aspects, only bad choices. Regarding your life and choices, you get to be the judge.

Sextile

A sextile aspect, also referred to as a *buried trine,* is indicated by a 60° angle with an orb no bigger than 5.7°. Just like trines, sextiles are also based on multiples of three and thus *synergy* and *harmony* is also the key theme. However given the close proximity, sextile placements are only relative to each other through *duplicity.* In this way, synthesis is not as natural or effortless as a trine.

Due to their availability, sextles are very easy to work with. A distinction to be made is that *sextiles must be worked with.* Unlike a trine, a sextile will take your conscious effort to develop. Given the accessibility, you will probably be pleased with the results your efforts yield. As it is the same basic shape, sextiles can also suffer the same negatives of trines. In addition to not being *particularly trying,* sextiles specifically may go unnoticed entirely and thus not developed at all.

Minor Aspects

The first five aspects we covered are considered the *Major Aspects.* These aspects were considered to be the most significant to the astronomer Claudius Ptolemy. However, basic geometry tells us that there are *far more shapes.* Theoretically, there are an infinite number of shapes because there are infinite *degrees between degrees.* As the major aspects will take some time to get used to, we won't go over all the minor ones. When you reach a level of comfort with the majors, check out semi-sextile, semi-square, sesqui-quadrate, quincunx, and quintile aspects (if you feel so inclined).

It is also worth mentioning that planets within charts may be *unaspected.* When a planet has no defined aspects, its relationship to other planets may not always be clear. Unaspected placements usually act as "loose cannons" and seem to operate independent of other elements. In these circumstances, we analyze

Simplified Astrology - 156

the qualities of the sign, the house position, and the surrounding aspects.

Aspect Patterns

Not to be confused with *planetary patterns,* aspect patterns are the *bigger picture* to consider when analyzing a chart. In this context, aspect pattern refers to three or more planets creating a distinct shape with their points in the wheel. Just like the basic major and minor aspects, these patterns can be created at the time of your birth, in transit, or between the planets of the people in your life (relative to yours).

This is an intermediate concept so really take your time here. There are many patterns to consider and they all speak volumes. When analyzing patterns in your own chart or for others: always keep in mind sign placement, house position, resonance of involved planets, and *other aspects in the chart.* When you get the hang of this, you can search for planetary patterns as well. In short this is the same thing as aspect patterns, but with the zodiac signs *removed.* When you analyze the placement of planets separate from the signs, you can see different elements of their relationships due to aspect and house position. This information is otherwise not considered, largely as it requires quite a solid understanding of astrology. You may not resonate with this material right now, but it

Simplified Astrology - 158

will take you to the next level when you are ready. Working with these patterns provides insight only to those with a trained eye.

T-Square

According to the Astro Databank, the T-Square is the most commonly formed aspect pattern, occurring in roughly 62% of charts. As the name suggests, a T-square is formed with squares *but also an opposition.* This is what gives the pattern it's "T" shape. Given that it is a combination of these two aspects, there is much to be said. The square portions of this pattern can be a cause for much discomfort or conflict but the opposition offers a direct route for one to channel their energy.

In all circumstances, a T-square will indicate some sort of *pressure.* Pressure can create diamonds or it can destroy structure. Consequently, this aspect can prove to be equally challenging and rewarding. As indicated by the squares, this is an opportunity to learn. T-squares may show areas in which an individual feels inclined to develop their skills. As the majority of people have a T-square in their chart, we see this is the source of many breakthroughs or frustrating limitations. In transit, *everyone* will experience this aspect at some point. Regardless if you were aware

Simplified Astrology - 159

of it or not, you were always interacting with these aspects, and you always will be.

Stellium

This pattern comes with a long list of technical rules but the premise is quite simple. This is a conjunction of three or more planets. There is much debate in the astrological community as to how big the orbs should be or what planets are considered to create a stellium. The Sun, Mercury, and Venus may sometimes be excluded from a stellium as their aspects are very close. At most Mercury can only be 28° away from the Sun, and Venus can be no more than 47° away. For this reason, it is very easy to create a stellium with these three bodies.

It seems everyone can agree on stelliums that are formed with three placements in the *same sign* or *same house.* As with all of our aspects: the tighter the orb, the stronger the influence of the pattern. A stellium indicates a concentration of energy. As always, there are positive and negatives attributes to this positioning. Stelliums create high focus in the area in which they are located. For many, a stellium may come with a sense of purpose or help one discover meaning in their life. In most cases, stelliums can

Simplified Astrology - 160

assist an individual in creating a wide array of skills in a specific area.

On the negative side, a stellium can be where a lack of balance stems from, due to the high concentration of a specific energy. There is also an inherent risk with *putting all your eggs in one basket.* Our interests will also show our vulnerabilities. In transit, stelliums can be especially volatile as they are a condensed group of trigger-points. Activating these trigger points may have a cascading effect in an individual's life.

No two stelliums are the same. When analyzing this pattern consider the amount of planets, the planets in question, house position, the size of orbs, the background of the individual, and the choices of said individual.

Grand Trine

Following in sequence, the Grand Trine is the third most common aspect pattern. A grand trine occurs between three trine (120°) placements, rather than just two. This position forms a complete equilateral triangle. By adding the third point to a trine aspect, the shape is completed and the energy can flow between each vertex with ease. The grand trine brings things full circle (as

Simplified Astrology - 161

it adds up to 360°) and may reveal areas of talents, gifts, and equilibrium.

As a grand trine only occurs in signs of the same element, we have a clue for deciphering them within a chart. The grand trine indicates the ability to harmonize the modalities of a specific element. As the focus of this angle is on *ease,* this is also not a particularly difficult aspect. This pattern is notorious for making things just easy enough to not feel the need to exert oneself. When utilized correctly, this pattern can be the source of many opportunities and benefits. At worst this can be a mechanism for self-sabotage, namely through isolation and complacency. Areas worth paying attention to regarding the grand trine are: *element, planet, house position,* and *penetrating aspects.*

Yod

A Yod is a pattern which forms an isosceles triangle within a chart. Specifically, this aspect is formed when two quincunx (150°) angles are connected by a sextile (60°) base. This positioning is often referred to as *The Finger of Fate* or *The Finger of God.* I find these titles to be unnecessarily ominous. As this pattern contains minor aspects, it is very often misunderstood. The

Simplified Astrology - 162

quincunx angle tells us most of what we need to know about the Yod, as they occupy two of the three points.

The relation between quincunx elements is strange, to say the least. The 150° angle connects signs of different *elements, modalities,* and *duplicities.* Thus, there is almost nothing in common between the two points. This creates much tension. Through the parallel, energy is usually directed toward the apex of the triangle, opposite the sextile (which has a different duplicity). In this way, we see the Yod's connection to one's destiny. The tensions and pressures we face in life ultimately influence the direction we decide to take.

It must be noted, aspect patterns often require time to be noticed in an individual's life. In the case of the Yod, this may not be apparent until a person reaches their middle ages. Over time, *cause and effect* gradually expands our horizons but also limits our options. However slowly, the Yod urges us towards our growth. House position and the apex planet are especially important when considering this pattern.

This is a good stopping point for aspect patterns as I do not want to overload you with the details of minor aspects. There are many less-common patterns that can be found within a chart such as a Grand Cross, Mystic Rectangle, Kite, or Thor's Hammer.

Simplified Astrology - 163

Many sites will calculate this information for you, allow you to adjust orbs, and add or remove aspects in your chart as you wish. In the spirit of competition, I estimate this service will never become *less free* than it is right now. The resources available to us today are truly amazing. In my personal experience, even the astrological tools I paid for have always been well-worth the money they cost.

Synastry

This is the part I know you've been waiting for. I'm finally going to tell you what to do with his/her birth chart. Synastry is the study of interpersonal relationships based on astrological compatibility. You should be able to see that this is impossible to do without using the elements we have previously discussed, namely *aspects.*

Let it be known from the beginning, you can have a fruitful and enjoyable relationship with a person of *any Sun sign.* As we are an energetic mixture of our *whole* chart, our upbringing, and our choices; synastry cannot be found based on Sun signs alone. Do me a favor, please. When you next hear someone claim a sign is or isn't compatible with another, ask them why they think so. If their answer does not mention aspects, rulership, elements, or a body that *isn't* the Sun; make a mental note that they do not truly understand synastry. You can politely educate them, if you feel so inclined. Alternatively, you could also hit them with the *"Ummm... actually"* and give them a proper square lesson!

The easiest way to do synastry is to create a *synastry chart,* however you can do this process mentally with basic arithmetic. A synastry chart is simply when two charts are overlaid in order to

Simplified Astrology - 165

see their similarities and differences. Free will and choice again supersede any inclination of compatibility you may find through synastry. It doesn't matter that you found your "perfect astrological match" if they don't want to be with you, right? We must take a common sense approach to synastry and all of astrology. Before we go into detail, consider synastry may be examined between *any two people*, and thus should not be limited to romantic interests. Examine the synastry of *all of your relationships* and you will be surprised what you find!

Effectively, most people search for *harmony* in their relationships. I'm well aware that some people are not wired for harmony, but this is the exception to the rule. Bear in mind; relating to *any person* creates a metaphorical "ship" in which the two people can (astral) travel together (*and sail through esoteric waters*). This is the nature of *every* relation-ship. Consciously or unconsciously boarding a ship with someone comes with responsibilities, expectations, and objectives. Just as we should not set sail without a map, the right tools, and a loyal crew that also wants to go where we do *and* understands their duties on the boat; we must be intentional with those who we choose to invest our energy into. Anyone who has been in a canoe understands the frustration of paddling by yourself; or worse, paddling *against*

Simplified Astrology - 166

another's incorrect steering. The underlying point I am getting at is *don't kid yourself.* Actions will always speak louder than words, and "good" synastry is perfectly capable of hurting you and leaving you unfulfilled.

There are many different things to consider in synastry. As we are effectively comparing two *selves,* it is important to start with the inner planets. Specifically, the luminaries are often the most insightful. As the Sun represents our *individualized self* and the Moon indicates our *internal world* and *feelings,* these two elements are *foundational* in relationships. When comparing your Sun or Moon sign to that of another, we must look at the aspect that is formed with theirs.

Each planet is an element of *the self.* The connections between you and another person's planets will be as dynamic as the relationship you share. We can view our aspects with a person from a purely astrological perspective, but we should also view them relative to our intentions. A conjunction may imply *automatic harmony,* but manifest differently in one of your relationships. Using the Sun as an example, two Leos may experience conflict due to attempting to "out-shine" the other. The Sun in the sign of Leo desires to be *seen, felt, and appreciated.* The self-centered, fixated qualities may result in both natives of this

Simplified Astrology - 167

sign feeling *unappreciated.* Each one is expressing the same thing, yet it is not directly aimed at the other's needs - and thus, not harmonious.

Let's further illustrate this point. Moon square Moon *sounds* like a pretty bad thing, right? *It definitely can be!* But it can also be great! We will use the Moon in Aries and the Moon in Capricorn as an example. Inherently, this position represents a difference of emotion and reaction to the world with any two signs. The Aries Moon is largely *self*-centered, passionate, or impulsive in the world of *feeling.* The Capricorn Moon on the other hand is practical, calculated, or even a bit austere. In a relationship, this placement *could be* the cause of arguments and hurt feelings due to emotional misunderstanding. With patience and grace, this same aspect will teach both partners lessons on *emotional intelligence,* as well as bringing about a more intimate connection between the two. Time, intimacy, and effort will eventually wear away and "circle" the square.

As a solid shape (corresponding to elemental earth), a square can be a great foundation to build a relationship on top of. Both partners are guaranteed to learn, as each possesses something the other *lacks.* This is the intuitive premise behind calling your significant other "your rock", as they are the solid foundation on

Simplified Astrology - 168

which you can rely on in times of conflict. The aspects we have covered must be viewed in terms of "roughness" or "smoothness" in relationships. How well the results hold up to your expectations will allow you to deduce whether an aspect is "good" or "bad" for you and the person in question.

It can be argued that a trine is the most harmonious angle in synastry. This shape represents *effortless equality*, which has harmed no one I can think of. Duality exists in everything, whether we can see it or not. Even a trine can create negative circumstances from its expression. As a synergizing aspect, a trine is largely benefic and rarely challenging. In a relationship, a trine could indicate a lack of growth or meaning when two individuals have different intentions. On a similar note, sextiles will not benefit those who do not choose to develop them. I cannot emphasize this enough: *figuring out your own intentions and the intentions of your partner* will take you closer to compatibility than astrology will. Astrology will help - but be intentional with your actions.

Given that it is the closest planet to the Sun, you will want to pay special attention to Mercury. Mercury indicates how we use our rational mind; effectively how we think and speak. For want of clear, honest communication - you will prefer a "harmonious" aspect here. You may find individuals sharing conjunct, trine, or

Simplified Astrology - 169

sextile aspects between your natal Mercuries are easy to talk to. You may find you enjoy talking to these people, you think in similar ways, and it is easy for both of you to be understood. Consequently, square, opposite, or inconjunct aspects between natal Mercuries can be the cause of arguments, misunderstandings, and verbal fights. Persistence will teach the individuals of the rough aspects how to compromise and grow, but not without friction or frustration.

If any planet could predict synastry by itself, it would be Venus. As a force, Venus represents attraction. The positioning of Venus will indicate what we consider *beautiful* or *valuable,* and what we are willing to compromise with. Consciously or not, we want romantic relationships with those of similar *values.* To even consider taking someone out of your seventh house and moving them into your eighth and splitting assets with them - you should share some priorities at least.

The positive aspects between Venus signs can indicate mutual attraction, similar values, and compatible expressions of love. The inverse is also true with the more challenging aspects. Due to the attractive nature of Venus, the aspect between two individuals can indicate whether or not one will be receptive to the love and appreciation of the other. Similarities in Venus placement

Simplified Astrology - 170

also can be found in your ability to *like the same things.* Venus represents joy and happiness, so most of us will want a *nice angle* here. Like I mentioned earlier, not everyone values harmony or happiness. If that is the case with you, go find a Venus square or opposition and you will be in *absolutely miserable company!* What fun!

Second only to Venus, Mars is of *huge* significance in synastry. Mars represents our energy, our passions, our motivations, and our sex drive. At large, this is how we assert ourselves is a dominating, dividing, and conquering way. In a romantic relationship, you will want a pleasant Mars aspect (whatever that means to you). *When two Mars placements love each other...* they have *really good* sex, shared ambitions, and even friendly competition. When at odds, not so much (just use your imagination). Pay attention to your partner's Mars placement so you know how to handle them when they get mad also. *The better you know someone, the better you can treat them!*

Truthfully, every planet will be of importance when you do synastry. However given the size and shape of our solar system, you will find the inner planets to be the most significant. Your outer planets will effectively define more "generational" qualities, and consequently there is more than astrology to be considered in

Simplified Astrology - 171

their effects. Not only will you want to consider the factors in one's upbringing; you will want to consider their choices, values, priorities, and unspoken expectations of you in addition to astrological compatibility.

Aspects are the glue that ties astrology together, take your time when you look at them. Effectively, you will want to look at *every* aspect in your chart and the ones you care about. Don't limit yourself to congruent planets with synastry. There are millions of questions you can ask. How does the Sun relate to the Moon? What does Mars think of Venus? What aspect do the two Ascendant lines create? What's in their seventh house? What priorities are indicated by the houses? How are they working with Saturn's energy? Do I even like this person? If you don't ask yourself the right questions, you may never find the answers you're looking for.

Transits

Planetary transits must, at the very least, be *understood* to effectively work with astrology. "Transit" refers to a planet's path around the Sun in our solar system. Motion is a constant in our world - the transits have always been occurring and they always will be. It usually doesn't hurt to be aware of this process! Analyzing the transits is essentially the same thing as *synastry*, with a slight caveat. We are looking at the synastry of your past and present (or future) self.

I find starting with synastry is more fun and engaging as it shows *with people*, how planetary energies interact. The transits are far more important as they affect everyone *simultaneously*. You must have a working understanding of your own chart in order to determine how transits affect you before *even attempting* to see how they affect others. It can sound tricky, but this is as easy as checking the weather app on your phone.

Following the same trend we have throughout this entire book, you will want to focus your attention on the *fastest moving* bodies first as they trigger aspects the quickest. Start with the Moon, specifically. I would strongly recommend finding an app or website that lets you do this easily (or you could go for the

Simplified Astrology - 173

physical ephemeris if that's your style). The Moon changes sign every two to three days. Make note of what major aspects are formed between the *present Moon* and your *natal Moon.* If you like to journal, I suggest noting these aspects when you write your feelings, as such is the nature of the Moon.

Naturally, you just peel back the layers from here. Pay attention to how Mercury is affecting your mode of thought. Juggle that with your Moon. Are there any natal Mercury aspects being created? What about present aspects between the Moon and Mercury? Now what about the Sun in terms of *everyone's conscious awareness?* What connections can you make between all of that? Consider Venus relative to what you find enjoyable or what others currently consider valuable. Mars will indicate how willpower is manifested or used. Aspects are found between all of these moving parts.

This is the point in the solar system where changes occur at an increasingly slow rate moving further. The Jupiterian energy collectively *expands* whatever sign it's in. You should always keep your astrological houses in mind when doing transits for yourself; especially so for the outer planets. Regardless of what aspects Jupiter is currently making with your natal Jupiter; consider what sign Jupiter is presently transiting. In your own chart, pay special

Simplified Astrology - 174

attention to which house that sign falls under. This is where you can expect *to see* this transit play out in your life. But bear in mind - transits will hit every house because the Earth *sure loves to spin.*

From Saturn on forward, the changes are *astronomically slow.* Make sure you pay attention to *major life transits.* The Saturn return is a big one, and you may even see two or three of them in your lifetime. At large, the Saturn return is a physical crisis, for better or for worse. The Uranus opposition is also a crisis, in an energetic sense. The Chiron return around age 50 is a spiritual crisis, for want of a better word. All of the outer planets are perfectly capable of making major aspects with your natal placements - some of them just don't have the same opportunities that the others do.

The Lunar Cycle

Since you can't directly look at the Sun, I want you to pay special attention to the other luminary. Earth only has one Moon, which contrary to most planets is not normal. Having only one satellite definitely has its perks. Above everything else, the cycle is *very easy* to track. Unless it's too cloudy, you can go outside and see the Moon's phase and sign with your eyes when it's above the horizon. Also given that the Moon resonates with *water,* we can

Simplified Astrology - 175

notice its influence through our own bodies in the realm of our *feelings.*

There are thirteen lunar cycles throughout the course of a year. The various phases of the lunar cycle synchronize with our individual and collective rhythms. The lunar cycle always begins with the New Moon. In this phase, the Moon is dark and invisible to our eyes - as it does not reflect the Sun's rays back towards the Earth. As a reminder, the New Moon always shares the same zodiac sign as the Sun. Energetically speaking, this is a clean slate. From our perspective, the Moon is empty of light, empty of vibration, and empty of feeling. This doesn't mean we won't have any feelings, however. In this state the Moon is at its lightest and most free, as the waning (shedding) process brings us to *New.*

Largely, New Moons are a great time to plant seeds - literally and metaphorically speaking. Directly after the new phase, the Moon begins waxing or filling up. Following the crescent pattern, the Moon gradually fills itself with light from the Sun and sends it our way. Energetically, this part of the process is about *growth* and *gain.* The two weeks after the New Moon are a time for taking action and watering and tending to our seeds. Just as the waxing moon indicates our satellite is gaining solar attention, this

Simplified Astrology - 176

process also indicates an emotional buildup (for better or worse) in our own bodies.

After two weeks of waxing we reach a climax. This is the Full Moon. The Moon is done eating and needs a to-go box. When your stomach is full of light you might as well digest it. Given that the Moon is *fulfilled*, it won't take on any more vibrations. Same will be said for our emotional worlds - at large. This is why Full Moons are so volatile. Collectively, we lack the mental and emotional space to handle our everyday resistances. In the case of emergencies, things really hit the fan around this time.

It is during the Full Moon that we can examine the quality of the seeds we have planted. Our emotions during the Full Moon will indicate whether we are bearing good or bad fruit. The heightened emotional sensitivity brought about by this stage of the cycle can be great for introspection. The thoughts and feelings we carry during this time are often the results of our intentions during the New Moon or waxing stages. We already know that statistics can get weird here. I want to illustrate this process for you, because we already know there's a link between Full Moons and crime.

Let's say somebody slaps your mom. In her face. *Really hard.* Just for this example: let's say you love your mom, *and this isn't cool.* You already didn't like this certain somebody for

Simplified Astrology - 177

whatever reason, but now it's personal. Your momma got slapped *right before the New Moon.* So around this time, you hear about it and think "I literally might just kill so-and-so". The thoughtform was born and thus the seed was planted.

But you won't really kill them. Murder is illegal and because your mom may not run the risk of getting slapped again immediately, it would definitely be pre-meditated and *not self-defence.* So naturally, you may brush the idea aside. But you aren't any less mad about it! In the waxing stage of the lunar cycle you may replay scenarios in your head - imagining your mom being hurt. These images will fill you with anger, assuming you really do love your mom. That's your family, and picking a fight with her included you. All the emotions you feel regarding this scenario will be built up during the cycle; all the anger, the guilt, the sadness, the *rage.*

Depending on how imaginative you are, you may mentally play out *actually killing them* in your mind. This is technically a psychic attack - because everything is real on some level (energetically). I digress slightly only to indicate that these thoughts are harmful for everyone involved. But in the spirit of *eye for an eye,* you probably wouldn't care. It's your mom we're talking about. In our example, I'm gonna suggest that you were

Simplified Astrology - 178

able to *get over it* during the final waxing stages - or at least stop giving them your attention. This is good. Being so angry can be exhausting. Truly, anger is self-inflicted punishment for someone else's behavior.

But then the Full Moon rolls around. *Something happens.* You see a text, a post on social media, *someone else's mom gets slapped,* or maybe you run into *them.* Suddenly you are reminded of what occurred to your mother. In this moment, *all of the emotions* come back but something is different. The pain, the blinding rage, and the desire is all still there - but much harder to contain. Given the emotional encumberment - you may not be able to handle these negative emotions this time. Before the reminder, *you already felt emotional.* Everyone is feeling this way around the Full Moon. At this time, our emotions should be *fulfilled.* Because of the bad seeds you planted earlier in the cycle, you may feel as if *right now* - killing that person would give you the satisfaction or fulfillment you are subconsciously seeking. This is why "bad things" happen around the Full Moon. People carry bad intentions regularly, but just can't help acting on them when they are too full of water. If it's high tide - you might need to run for your safety.

So really, there is nothing inherently good or bad about the Moon and it's cycles. Again, we are falling back on the choices

Simplified Astrology - 179

you make. It's your life, so only *you* (or your government) can judge you. It's very beneficial to be aware of the lunar cycle so you can align your intentions with it. Full Moons are also significant in the fact that they always oppose the Sun. This opposition is the same reason the Moon is actually seen as "full". This aspect also makes this part of the cycle more challenging on a collective level. The opposition creates either a bridge or a disconnect between the conscious awareness (Sun) and the reactions to the world (Moon) at large.

The heightened awareness or sensitivity brought about by Full Moons marks them as a powerful time for inner-work and growth. Many people like to set lunar goals. When the Moon is Full, subtraction should be the focus. Immediately following the full stage, the Moon begins waning, or shedding the light and vibrations it picked up earlier. This is a time of *release.* The waning moon is the easiest time to let go of what no longer serves you. When all the releasing has been completed, our Moon starts fresh at *new* in the same sign as the Sun.

Consider what phase the Moon was in when you were born. This also has a significance regarding your personality!

Simplified Astrology - 180

Moon Void of Course

This is an interesting phenomenon regarding the lunar cycle. Due to the rapid pace of the Moon, our satellite shifts sign position every 2-3 days. Collectively, the sign the Moon is under will show us how humanity *feels* and *responds* to the world (when translated through our own natal alignments). Keeping the decanates in mind, we know the transition between two signs is gradual. Regardless of the zodiac signs *assigned modality* - we can witness cardinal, fixated, and mutable qualities of each sign as a planet moves through it.

This is fine and dandy. But with the Moon there arises a problem between the *mutable dispelling* and the next *cardinal wave.* After the Moon makes its last major aspect in one sign - it will spend some time *in between signs* and will usually be unaspected. This is what we call *void of course.* Due to the rate of the lunar cycle, the Moon can be *stuck in between* signs for a matter of minutes or even several hours!

These time periods are very unstable at large. Luckily, void of course doesn't last very long. Because the Moon directly influences our water & emotions, many can actually *feel* when the Moon switches sign. It generally doesn't feel good. Things *just*

Simplified Astrology - 181

don't feel right. The stability is not there and the emotional world is largely confusing during VOC. I encourage you to challenge everything I present to you in this book. *Don't let me tell you what to do.* What I will say about VOC is that many astrologers advise against making important decisions during these times.

Given the way you feel, you may want to do nothing more than relax when the Moon makes these shifts. The Moon goes void of course many times a week, therefore much information has been compiled regarding this phenomenon. Metaphorically - this is a time where you *don't* want to plant seeds. This is a guideline, so again *do not let astrology limit your personal power.* Plant if you must. Statistically speaking, void of course coincides with canceled appointments, harmful contracts, misunderstandings, candidates *not* getting elected, and irrational emotional actions and reactions. If you can, avoid making significant decisions until the Moon finds its way into the next sign. Use these times to reflect, relax, organize, and enjoy yourself.

When you check transits for yourself or others, there is much to consider and much to disregard. I implore you to keep your intentions in mind and make use of your resources. Stay flexible and pursue anything you find meaningful in the vast world of astrology. I believe over time you will be impressed with this tool and what you can do with it. Thank you for taking this journey with me. In the name of correspondence, you are a star and I can't wait to see what lights you bring to the universe.

Planetary Hours

This section is a bonus for the *magickally inclined* that want to use correspondence on a deeper level and direct some energy. Since the times of ancient Egypt, the planetary bodies were superimposed on the calendar and within the hours of the day. *Most of magick is preparation.* Educating yourself and adding layers of correspondence builds up energy for whatever work you are doing. *Timing is very important.* Planetary hours are an old concept so we want to make sure we do them correctly. Sure, we have apps and calculators now - but if we can't check the math how do we know they're right?

To calculate planetary hours, you must know which planet rules each day of the week. This is listed in the *Tables of Correspondence* section. Simply put, the planetary ruler of the day rules the first hour of said day. The next planet rules over the next hour in sequence until we end up at the 7th planet, or the first one we started at. The cycle then repeats. This is the general concept but it's not that cut and dry.

Essentially, daytime is split into twelve equal "planetary hours" and so is nighttime. Planetary hours are not the same as our 60-minute hours so some calculation is required. The calculator on

Simplified Astrology - 184

your phone and Google will give you all the information you need. Effectively, you need to know what time the Sun rises and sets for the day in question. Google this, and you will immediately get the correct information based on your IP address. If you use a VPN, make sure your location is accurate.

Next you will want to work out how many minutes there are between sunrise and sunset. Let's just say on a specific Tuesday, the Sun rises at 6:43am and sets at 7:30pm. The numbers are arbitrary so just follow the example. This one is actually almost easy enough to do mentally. The Sun sets almost exactly 13 hours after sunrise - but we have to subtract off the extra 13 minutes. 13 x 60 = 780; 780 - 13 = 767.

We have concluded that on this day there are 767 minutes of *daytime*. 767 / 12 = 63.91.

Each *planetary hour* of this day will be almost 64 minutes long. Given the season you are living through based on geography, your planetary hours can be either shorter or longer than regular hours. Many grimoires or *books of shadows* will call for you to perform work during certain hours. Being able to calculate these for yourself gives you the peace of mind knowing that you have prepared properly.

Working with the current example, Mars rules the first hour of the day starting at 6:43am. Mars continues to rule this "hour" for 63.91 minutes. At 7:47am, the second planetary hour begins and is ruled by Mercury, the next planet in sequence. We continue with these same intervals and follow the order of the rulers of the days of the week.

The calculations of planetary hours are quite easy when you do this at least once. To further illustrate - let's say you want to perform a spell or ritual that requires to be done in the 7th planetary hour of the day. This is very simple math. To ensure that you begin your magickal working *at the beginning of the 7th planetary hour*, you want to know what time that hour starts. Using the same day, we need to calculate how many hours pass before the time in question. That's six complete planetary hours. On this day, the planetary hours are 63.91 minutes, so we will multiply that figure by 6. 63.91 x 6 = 383.46 minutes.

The hour we wish to work in is exactly 383.46 minutes after sunrise. To put this figure on the clock, we have to translate it. Divide by 60 so you know how many normal hours this is. 383.46 / 60 = 6.391 hours. The 6 part is simple, but how many minutes is .391 hours? This is very easy. Multiply .391 by 60 and you'll get the exact answer. This is 23.46 minutes - let's just call it

Simplified Astrology - 186

23 and a half. Six hours and 23.5 minutes from sunrise on this day (6:43am) is 1:06pm (and about 30 seconds). In this example, I would shoot for setting up your tools right around 1pm - you should begin right around the start of the planetary hour with ample time to spare.

If you are *magickally inclined,* don't stop here. Add as many correspondences to your work as you possibly can. Opt for a compliant moon phase, planetary alignment, and corresponding colors/incenses/metals. If you aren't the ritual magick type, you can still buy your lottery tickets in a Venus or Jupiter hour (on Thursday or Friday). While I wouldn't recommend wasting your money like this - I want you to realize how these hours can be used to direct energy. Get creative.

Planetary hours are another tool only limited by your understanding. Everything in our universe is energy. You are responsible for how you direct your own energy and the energies you have access to. I implore you: *know thyself,* be intentional with your life, and if it harms none - *do what thou wilt.*

Simplified Astrology - 187

Acknowledgements

First and foremost - this book is dedicated to my mother, Paula. Thank you for raising me with so much love, encouraging me to keep an open mind, and teaching me to take responsibility for my ideas. I appreciate all that you have done for me. Thank you for exposing me to the depths of the eighth and the ninth. I love that I have someone so close to me whom I can speak this language with.

Equal praise must be given to my father, Michael. A man who exemplifies the teachings of Saturn. You taught me the value of hard work and *consistency*. You are my role-model and my rock. I am eternally grateful that you provided for my needs and gave me the stability to pursue what matters to me. You continue to support me on every step of my journey and that means everything to me. I know in my spirit that you love me unconditionally and no matter what; you will help me *work the problem*. It's written in our synastry chart, too.

Special thanks to my friend Ginger. You were the first one to introduce me to the concept of the natal chart, and thus my journey truly began. In addition to expanding my horizons, you helped me feel recognized - in a spiritual sense. I know *you know;*

Simplified Astrology - 188

the higher up you go in consciousness - the fewer people there are. Elevation can be lonely, so thank you for making it less lonely! You are a true leader and it's impossible not to notice your love for your community. I value every minute I've spent meeting with you!

And to my friend, Paxton: thank you for your shining influence in my life. Whether you realize it or not, you greatly expedited my learning process of astrology. Your wisdom, your love, and your care for this world is unmatched! I say in the most respectful way possible - you are a dangerous individual! I admire how fluidly you travel between the 6th and 12th. You already overstand how this world works and I can't wait to take pride in your future accomplishments!

And to Bill Duvendack: you're a wizard, dude. I love the way your mind works and I appreciate your skill as a teacher. You were the first professional astrologer I ever met and your passion affirmed to me: *there is definitely something here.* You also expedited my learning process. Your ability to synthesize connections and eloquently explain *the occult* is admirable, to say the very least. I look forward to your future classes and books.

Simplified Astrology - 189

About The Author

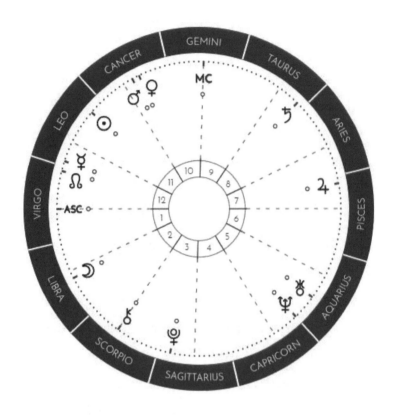

Mark Meyer
07/29/1998 9:30AM
St. Louis, MO
Placidus
Via astro-charts.com

Simplified Astrology - 190

Notes

Simplified Astrology - 191